THE LIBRARY OF CONTEMPORARY THOUGHT

America's most original voices
tackle today's most provocative issues

VINCENT BUGLIOSI

NO ISLAND OF SANITY

Paula Jones v. Bill Clinton:
The Supreme Court on Trial

"By the time readers finish this book I'm confident that most of them will be highly condemnatory of the Supreme Court, some even angry at the Court, for its ruling in the Paula Jones case. . . .

"The highest court in our land made an incomprehensible and terribly flawed decision against the nation's most powerful and important citizen, one that has injurious ramifications for all of us. . . .

"What conceivable argument could possibly be made for the proposition that Jones's right to proceed to trial now with her private lawsuit is more important than the public's right to have its president be undiverted and undistracted in the performance of his duties running the country? No one answered that question in the Jones case for the simple reason that *it was never even asked.*"

Also by Vincent Bugliosi

Helter Skelter (with Curt Gentry)
Till Death Us Do Part (with Ken Hurwitz)
And the Sea Will Tell (with Bruce Henderson)
The Phoenix Solution: Getting Serious About Winning America's Drug War
Outrage: The Five Reasons Why O.J. Simpson Got Away With Murder

NO ISLAND
OF SANITY

Paula Jones v. Bill Clinton:
The Supreme Court on Trial

VINCENT BUGLIOSI

THE LIBRARY OF CONTEMPORARY THOUGHT
THE BALLANTINE PUBLISHING GROUP • NEW YORK

The Library of Contemporary Thought
Published by The Ballantine Publishing Group

Copyright © 1998 by Vincent Bugliosi

Library of Congress Cataloging-in-Publication Data
Bugliosi, Vincent.
No island of sanity : Paula Jones v. Bill Clinton : the Supreme Court on trial /
Vincent Bugliosi. — 1st ed.
p.   cm.
ISBN 0-345-42487-5 (alk. paper)
1. Jones, Paula, 1966– —Trials, litigation, etc.   2. Clinton, Bill, 1946– —
Trials, litigation, etc.   3. Sexual harassment—Law and legislation—
United States.   I. Title.
KF228.J66B84   1998
342.73'0878'0269—dc21   97-50261
CIP

Text design by Holly Johnson
Cover design by Ruth Ross
Photo illustration by Ruth Ross based on a photo by
Joseph Pobereskin/Tony Stone Images, NY

Manufactured in the United States of America

First Edition: February 1998

10   9   8   7   6   5   4   3   2   1

To those fellow Americans who respect and are concerned about the office of the presidency, irrespective of the political affiliation of its temporary occupants

PART ONE

A Rather Long and Discursive Dissertation
to Prepare the Reader for the Shocking
Revelation (and Make the Reader More
Receptive than He or She Would Normally Be
to Agreeing with the Charge) that the
U.S. Supreme Court in the Paula Jones Case
Made a Ruling that Was Less Profound
than What We Could Expect of Even
a Layperson of Below-Average Intelligence

As the expression goes when two people of opposite gender keep bumping into each other in different places, "We have to stop meeting like this, or else people will start talking about us." Likewise, I have to stop pointing out to the American public things they never saw, otherwise people are going to start saying, as the *Newsday* review said of *Outrage*, my book on the O.J. Simpson case, "Is everybody wrong but Bugliosi? Well, he makes a darned conclusive argument that this is so."

What *Newsday* was referring to was a rather remarkable thing. Prior to the hardcover publication of *Outrage: The Five Reasons Why*

O.J. Simpson Got Away with Murder on June 10, 1996, no one, but no one, was blaming the prosecution for the not-guilty verdict in the Simpson case and pointing out their unbelievable incompetence. Although that incompetence (in many instances it went beyond incompetence into the area of unprecedented, unheard of, bizarre, unique) took place right before the eyes of millions and millions of television viewers—including thousands of trial lawyers—in the most publicized murder trial in American history, the overwhelming consensus was that the prosecution did all they could possibly do and the jury was completely responsible for what happened. (Those few who didn't say this claimed that the LAPD botched the case for the prosecution before it came to trial.)

As *Newsweek* told its readers on September 30, 1996, "It is accepted wisdom that prosecutors lost the criminal trial virtually the day the predominantly African-American jury was sworn in." Yes, the accepted "wisdom" of all those who haven't read *Outrage*. But as the *Los Angeles Times* said in its review, "No one who reads this book will ever again believe that the most publicized acquittal in the history of American jurisprudence was solely the result of juror prejudice or the machinations of unscrupulous defense attorneys. The D.A. and the prosecutors have been called before the Bar of Justice." The *New York Times Book Review* said that *Outrage* "puts the blame where it belongs."

Although *Outrage* is a very harsh indictment of the prosecutorial effort in the Simpson case, if there's one thing I take pride in, it's that I never, ever make a charge without supporting it. You might not agree with me, but I invariably offer, as I will do in this book, an enormous amount of support for my position. How often do you read a declarative, assertive statement in the caption or first paragraph of an article and then search in vain in the article for the support? Either it's not there or the support is anemic. That's not my style. And in *Outrage* I offer page after page, example after example of incompetence so extreme that readers can only shake their head and say to themselves, "How can this possibly be?" and "Why didn't I see this?"

Let me say that the jury in the Simpson case was bad; major, big-time bad. The prosecutors were even worse, however. But as bad as the prosecutors were, people tend to forget that on the first ballot back in the jury room, a black juror and a white juror voted guilty. If you can get a ten-two vote on the first ballot with an extremely inferior performance, you can imagine, by extrapolation, what would have happened if there had been an A-plus performance by the prosecution, which the people of the State of California were entitled to. I'm personally convinced that even this jury would have responded with a guilty verdict, or at an absolute minimum, a hung jury.

Because of the prosecution's staggering incompetence in the Simpson case[1] (one example among a hundred: Simpson admitted to the police that he was dripping blood on the night of the murders but said he had "no idea" how he got cut, yet unbelievably the prosecutors never offered this evidence to the jury), instead of Simpson now being in the general prison population at San Quentin or on death row, he plays golf every day, and with a smile on his face. Yet, prior to *Outrage*, no book, no magazine article, no talking head (the lawyer-commentators who babbled endlessly on TV during the trial) had noted this extreme incompetence. (Alan Dershowitz, in his book *Reasonable Doubts*, was the only one who even said that the prosecution *contributed* to the result, but Dershowitz doesn't mention any of the tremendous number of enormous blunders set forth in *Outrage*, and the main mistake Dershowitz claims the prosecution made—calling Mark Fuhrman to the stand—wasn't a blunder at all. They had no choice *but* to call him. If they hadn't, the defense would have. Since the defense built its entire, outrageous case around him, they would have gotten him up on that witness stand if they had to carry him up there on a stretcher.) Just two examples: Jeffrey Toobin, a lawyer and Harvard law graduate, covered the trial for the *New Yorker*. Yet even though he is an intelligent man and a fine writer, Toobin apparently saw absolutely nothing of the prosecutors' extreme incompetence that was taking place before his very eyes. In his October 16, 1995, wrap-up article, *before* publication of *Outrage*, not only doesn't he criticize the prosecution's performance in any way whatsoever, but he writes: "It is difficult to imagine how else [Marcia] Clark might have tried her case . . . there appears to have been no one thing the prosecution could have done—or undone— that would have changed the result in this case. . . . The result, it now seems, was preordained." He describes Clark as being "at times brilliant." But as the review of Toobin's later book on the case, *The*

Run of His Life (which came out five months after *Outrage* was published), in the *New York Times Book Review* on September 19, 1996, points out, Toobin suddenly found all types of problems with the prosecution's performance. The reviewer wrote: "Mr. Toobin may claim that the inadequacies of Ms. Clark and Mr. Darden were revealed only gradually, but in his book he criticizes Ms. Clark at the same stages of the trial during which he praised her in his magazine pieces. For example, his glowing profile of her was published shortly after what the book describes as her disastrous, misguided jury selection, which he implies may have lost the case. Of course, he is entitled to change his mind, *but without any explanation** his divergent reports raise questions about his credibility. You want to put him under oath and cross-examine him."

Most of the talking heads were known only to their immediate families and friends prior to the Simpson trial. An exception was Joe Di Genova, a bright and articulate lawyer and former prosecutor who previously had been the U.S. attorney in Washington, D.C., and who is a respected member of the legal profession. But after the verdict, when the *L.A. Times* asked me and three other prosecutors, including Di Genova, to write a statement on how we would have handled the case differently, I set forth some of what I later stated in *Outrage*, where I point out the astounding, shocking, and incredible errors made by the prosecutors. But Di Genova, who has said he watched every day of the trial on television, wrote: "I don't have an answer to that question." He added: "I think they did a damn good job under horrible circumstances." In other words, as far as Di Genova was concerned, the prosecutors in the Simpson case did all they possibly could. But Di Genova can now be heard on TV talking about the "unbelievable incompetence" of the prosecutors in the Simpson case.

If Joe Di Genova and Jeffrey Toobin and others didn't learn about the prosecution's incompetence from *Outrage* (from their own lips, we know they certainly didn't learn about it from their having watched the trial), from whom did they learn it? Did some anonymous person come up to them in a bar, tap them on the shoulder, and say, "Listen, you don't know who I am, but here's the skinny on

---

*All emphasis by italics in this book is provided by the author, unless otherwise indicated.

what went down in the Simpson case," and they took out their pads and pencils and started writing furiously?

This will undoubtedly sound boastful, but it all started with *Outrage*. The book, and the word of mouth it produced, changed the perception of many Americans about the Simpson case.

The reason why I've discussed the Simpson case and why I'm going to make several other observations that, at least at first blush, are unrelated to the Supreme Court's decision in the Paula Jones case is that I hope they all will set the stage for, and help the reader more readily accept and understand, what I in due time will prove to you in this book: that the U.S. Supreme Court made an egregiously erroneous ruling in the Paula Jones case against the president of the United States, and that, unbelievably, as in the Simpson case, no one, at least no one I'm aware of, saw the terrible legal error they made.

Perhaps even more strangely—and this is nothing short of remarkable—I have yet to read one single article, anywhere, *criticizing* the Supreme Court for its ruling in the case. (In fact, as we will see later on, even many who were upset with the Court's ruling and regretted its potential adverse implications went on to conclude that the Court was nevertheless legally correct in its ruling.) But by the time readers finish this book I'm confident that most of them will be highly condemnatory of the Supreme Court, some even angry at the Court, for its ruling in the Paula Jones case.

About no one else seeing the error: Let me qualify this. I would guess that some constitutional law professors, somewhere, saw it. But I can tell you who didn't—no one in the media that I'm aware of, including the major newspapers of the land and political pundits, saw it. The president's own lawyer, Robert S. Bennett, didn't see it. Much more important, the Supreme Court of the United States, which handed down the ruling, didn't see it. As a result, the highest court in our land made an incomprehensible and terribly flawed decision against the nation's most powerful and important citizen, one that has injurious ramifications for all of us.

It should be noted off the top that the position taken in this book has nothing at all to do with being pro-Clinton or pro-Democrat. It has everything to do with the office of the presidency of the United States. In fact, during Watergate, with a Republican president, I became so upset with people treating the matter as though it was so much more serious than it really was (prosecutor Leon Jaworski, incredibly, analogized it to the Third Reich, which resulted, as we know, in fifty million deaths during World War II, including the six million Jews murdered during the Holocaust) and with politicians (who, if the truth be told, had covered up their own misconduct) reacting with phony horror over the president's malfeasances (e.g., Senator Ted Kennedy, who did everything within his power to suppress the facts of Chappaquiddick) that I wanted to write a book titled *Watergate: America's Finest Hour of Hypocrisy*, but prior commitments prevented me from doing so.

I believe I can establish conclusively that the Supreme Court's decision in this case was terribly and demonstrably wrong. The reason is that the Court failed to balance, as it must always do, the public interest against the private interest; here, the public interest in the effective functioning of the office of the presidency against the private interest of Paula Jones to have her case heard, without further delay, during the president's term in office. One could perhaps say that because I am not a constitutional scholar or even an appellate lawyer, just a plain trial lawyer, I am out of my depth in taking on the highest court in the land in this case. But in this instance, the *Jones v. Clinton* case, the depth is so shallow that anyone using even an ounce of common sense could navigate its weak currents. This is not the type of situation where the Supreme Court has issued a ruling with which those who disagree question the Court's analysis and interpretation of the legal issues before it. This happens every day; people see things differently all the time. This is a situation where, for instance, the judge of a professional fight never even added up his scorecard correctly, giving only one point, instead of the two he should have, to a knockdown in the third round. In other words, this is a ruling that is fatally defective, one no rational person can fail to condemn once he or she becomes aware of what the Supreme Court actually did in this case. The error was so flagrant that virtually everyone *should* have seen it. But they didn't.

And that leads me, before we get into a fairly detailed examination of the Court's decision, into a discussion of two prefatory matters, the first of which is to try to explain why no one whom I'm aware of has been talking about the Supreme Court's terrible blunder in the Paula Jones case (and by extension, why no one saw the incompetence of the prosecutors in the Simpson case). The second concerns a frightening reality about the direction of American life.

The most plausible explanation of why no one saw the Supreme Court's blunder is that there is a curious phenomenon among human beings: Most people usually see what they expect or want to see, not what is actually in front of them. And no one can be faulted for assuming that the highest court in the land knows what the law is and therefore must have known what they were doing in the Paula Jones case.[2]

I believe it was Thoreau who spoke of the endless struggle to see what is right before our eyes. I don't think I'm a particularly bright individual, but there are two qualities I long ago learned I did possess. One is the ability to separate the wheat from the chaff, to see through to the core of a problem, usually very quickly. The second, related quality (one that I have found is even more rare, and again has nothing to do with intelligence) is that when I read, see, or hear anything, for some reason I am totally uninfluenced by what has been previously said or written about the subject. I am able to form impressions simply on the basis of what I see taking place in front of me. I'd like to relate a few examples to illustrate the point I am making here. One example among many I could give concerns the Czech tennis great, Ivan Lendl. In the early years of his sterling career, Lendl was a quitter. If things were going well, he'd steamroll over his opponents, but if they got tough, oftentimes he'd give up. In the finals of one U.S. Open years ago, he was facing Jimmy Connors, who doesn't know what the term "give up" even means. At some point in the match, Lendl, unbelievably, stopped running after balls that were any distance away from him and lost ingloriously to Connors. I was very angry. How dare Lendl give up? He's in the finals of the second most important tennis tournament in the world (Wimbledon is normally considered to be the premier event in the sport), and he wasn't giving it his all? If he didn't personally care, didn't he owe it to the millions of people watching the event on TV? And if he didn't even care about them, didn't he at least owe it to the great game of tennis?

After the match I went to the courts to play. I was still fuming and voiced my displeasure with Lendl to no fewer than four or five of the players at the court who had also seen the match, saying that Lendl should be suspended and barred from playing in any sanctioned tennis tournament for at least a year. None of them knew what I was talking about. They hadn't noticed anything unusual about Lendl's performance at all. And the reason, of course, is that these were players who, like me, are willing to crash into a fence to retrieve a ball. And that's where nothing is at stake other than to satisfy our pea brain's atavistic desire to win. If we will knock ourselves out in a meaningless practice match, obviously when you're playing Jimmy Connors in the finals of the U.S. Open, you'll kill yourself to win, right?

My tennis colleagues simply didn't see what happened in the Connors-Lendl match. They saw what they expected to see. The next day not one of the accounts of the match I read in the newspapers mentioned Lendl's sorry and inexcusable performance, and there was no mention of his having sustained any injury during the match that would have caused it. I was happy to read, in an edition of *Sports Illustrated* a month or so later, that tennis greats Pancho Segura and Bobby Riggs, who were courtside during the match, were disgusted by Lendl's performance. It should be mentioned that during the middle and latter parts of Lendl's career, he developed into one of the grittiest, most tenacious, and competitive players on the tour, never saying die, as they say, until the fat lady sang.

Another sports example: When I was young, I was an avid boxing fan, but in recent years I rarely even have time to watch a closed-circuit fight. About two or so years ago I had been hearing about how great a fighter Oscar De La Hoya, the former Olympic champion from East Los Angeles, was, and his string of knockouts. The first time I saw him was in a few short snippets on the evening news, and I immediately noticed that he appeared to have no right hand. His left was almost his total offense, reminding me of former heavyweight champion Joe Frazier. A year or so later, at a friend's home, I finally watched a complete fight of De La Hoya's with a bunch of boxing aficionados. When I told them before the fight that De La Hoya apparently had no right hand, all of them told me I was wrong. They assured me that he "was a complete fighter." But they obviously were simply assuming this since he was undefeated and had all those knockouts. I told them to watch for his right hand in the upcoming fight. Sure enough, De La Hoya hadn't gotten any more snap and power in that hand since I'd seen the snippets on TV. My friends, without exception, were forced to agree with me that although he's a hell of a fighter, his right is weak. His new trainer may have taught him how to hit with his right by the time this book is published, but I'll give you one-hundred-to-one odds that in every single one of his knockouts up to this point, not one was with his right hand. From what I have seen of De La Hoya, he's almost a one-armed fighter.

Let's talk for a moment about this phenomenon in the political arena. We constantly hear from right-wing Republicans about the "liberal media." When they say this, they're clearly concerning themselves not with the fact that the members of the media are liberal (surveys consistently show that the majority of the media is, indeed, somewhat liberal in their political persuasion), but with the supposed fact that the media is soft on Democrats as opposed to Republicans *because* they are liberal. In other words, if the media is liberal, it stands to reason that they're going to be more partial to Democrats than Republicans. Theoretically, it sounds logical. But the reality is that it's an example of right-wing Republicans seeing what they expect to see, not what's really there. I'll give two examples to make my case. When I've pointed out to some acquaintances of mine on the political right how radio talk-show host Rush Limbaugh is nothing but a disgusting, two-bit shill for the right wing (not the moderate one) of the Republican Party, they immediately counter by comparing Limbaugh to several liberal members of the media, such as Los Angeles radio talk-show host Michael Jackson or CNN's Larry King. But there *is* no comparison. Although Jackson and King are liberal, they are perfect gentlemen on the air. Jackson is a highly civilized fellow who is respectful to all representatives of the political spectrum. And we all know that King is such a nice guy that he would have trouble being tough with the likes of Hitler or Stalin.

(I'm exaggerating, of course.) Right-wing figures such as Oliver North and G. Gordon Liddy (who has much more credibility than Limbaugh) are frequently on his show, and the exchanges are as friendly and pleasant as could be. In fact, one could listen to King for months without getting an inkling of his political bent. Not so with Limbaugh. He's made a career the past five years out of vilifying the president of the United States. It's almost impossible to listen to him for more than a few minutes without hearing a personal, mean-spirited, and highly derogatory tirade against, or ridicule of, President Clinton, his wife, Hillary, and the Democratic Party, including savaging their character and going so far as to impugn their patriotism. This he does day in and day out, demonstrating an infidelity to elementary decency that is astonishingly high. He has even had the audacious bad taste to attack, on his radio show, the physical appearance of Clinton's daughter, Chelsea, calling her "ugly." Another time, on his television show, after showing a photograph of Socks, the Clintons' cat, he asked his audience if they were aware that there was also "a White House dog," proceeding to then show them a photo of Chelsea. Limbaugh also has said that Hillary's face looks like "a Pontiac hood ornament." (When Limbaugh takes a momentary breather from slandering the Clintons, he can be heard uttering such delightful gems as this: "I'm sick and tired of playing the one phony game I've had to play, and that is this so-called compassion for the poor. I don't have compassion for the poor.")

Limbaugh says he is successful "because people are tired of being insulted elsewhere on the radio or television dial. They enjoy listening to someone who respects their intelligence." But even if one is conservative, how can any intelligent person *fail* to be deeply offended by Rush Limbaugh? The reason I say this is that although some of the things he says have merit, when it comes to politics, his favorite topic, he has absolutely no credibility at all. On any matter where there is a divergence between the Republican and Democratic positions, invariably, without exception, 100 percent of the time, he takes the Republican side. You know what he's going to say before he says it. For Limbaugh to have any credibility, the Republicans would *always* have to be right and the Democrats *always* wrong; the Republicans *always* the good people, the Democrats *always* the bad people. Since we know, of course, that this can't be true, he has no credibility, not one molecule, therefore, every thinking person should be offended by him. I don't know of anyone else in this country, even die-hard Republican politicians who oppose the president, even Jesse Helms, who is an absolute disgrace to the republic,[3] who is as unremitting and acerbic in his or her attacks on the Clintons and the Democratic Party. So there is no comparison between Rush Limbaugh and Larry King; yet right-wingers, because they see what they expect to see, think that King is the flip side of Limbaugh.[4]

Of course, Limbaugh is also a flag-waver. But the problem with Limbaugh and his ilk is that those who wear their patriotism on their sleeves usually have very little left inside. Predictably, Limbaugh was nowhere to be found during the Vietnam War, taking a college student deferment. Almost without exception (Oliver North is one exception who comes to mind, being a Vietnam war hero), the true patriots and American heroes—I'm speaking about people like Bob Dole, and Senators John Glenn, John McCain, and Bob Kerrey—are not jingoistic flag-wavers.

The reality is that although the right wing is absolutely insistent that the "liberal media" has been soft on President Clinton, they've actually been a lot harder on him than his Republican opposition, and this has been typical of the treatment he and his predecessors have been getting for years. (Again, this has nothing to do with the quality of Clinton's presidency. It has everything to do with perception, with seeing the reality of a situation. Why is it that most people who are opposed to President Clinton seem to be incapable of saying something like "I don't like President Clinton, but I think the press is very hard on him, obsessing on his alleged wrongs"? The first part of that statement is a subjective judgment of the president. The second part, however, is an objective fact. While everyone is entitled to their own opinion, they're not entitled to their own facts.) For example, in the 1992 presidential election campaign, between President Bush and Clinton, the allegation surfaced that Clinton had been a draft dodger in the Vietnam War. Whether he was or not wasn't 100 percent clear. Clinton is as elusive as mercury, and he managed to blur pretty effectively precisely what happened back then. However, the overriding consensus is that he had dodged the draft. But he was only twenty at the time, a private citizen, and at least if he was a draft dodger he had the courage to stand up and be counted against the war in Vietnam, publicly joining in protests and demonstrations against the most unpopular war in American history. Compare that to chest-thumping flag-wavers like Limbaugh and Newt Gingrich, who quietly avoided the draft. Or Dan Quayle, whose influential father was able to get him into the Indiana National Guard (ahead of others who were on the waiting list above him). As a result, Quayle spent the war right in the midst of the bombs, land mines, and flying grenades of war-torn Indianapolis. In any event, the press wrote articles about Clinton's avoiding the draft ad nauseam. Day after day after day it was a big story. Simultaneously, we had President Bush's probable involvement in the Iran-Contra affair, a scandal that not only involved the sale of arms to the terrorist nation of Iran in violation of both the National Security Act and the Arms Export Control Act, but, in using the proceeds to help fund the CIA-backed Contra rebels in their efforts to overthrow the Nicaraguan government, violated an explicit congressional prohibition ("the Boland Amendments") against such assistance.[5]

Among other evidence against Bush were the personal notes of President Reagan's secretary of defense, Caspar Weinberger. Those notes made it clear that, contrary to Bush's repeated claim that he was "out of the loop" on Iran-Contra, he was indeed in the loop. Weinberger's notes for a January 7, 1986, meeting in the Oval Office with President Reagan read: "The President decided to go with Israeli-Iranian offer to release our 5 hostages in return for sale of 4,000 TOW's to Iran by Israel. George Shultz [secretary of state] and I opposed—Bill Casey, Ed Meese and VP [Bush] favored—as did Poindexter." (Bush eventually pardoned Weinberger, who had been indicted for making false statements to Congress regarding Iran-Contra, before the latter's case came to trial; many felt this was done by Bush to avoid the proof that would have been elicited at the trial that he was a knowing participant in Iran-Contra.) Bush's role in Iran-Contra should have been a major, major story covered in penetrating depth by the media; after all, the scandal dealt with a serious violation of this nation's constitutional scheme of government, participated in by someone who was not, like Clinton, a private citizen barely out of his teens, but a mature adult who was the vice president of the United States. But Bush's involvement in the Iran-

Contra affair was dwarfed throughout the campaign by Clinton's supposed evasion of the draft.

To see the harsh treatment the "liberal media" give President Clinton and the Democrats, all one has to do is look at today's newspapers and the ridiculous coverage the media gave for over four months last year to the alleged campaign fund-raising abuses by the president, vice president, and Democratic Party—who were investigated, mind you, by the Republican Party, of all people. How insane can one get? For the Republicans to vigorously investigate the Democrats for the *identical* thing they do and have been doing for years takes audacity to symphonic and operatic levels.

The Republican Party, year in and year out, consistently raises much more money for presidential and congressional elections than the Democratic Party, and, as often as not, in just as dishonorable a way. But suddenly, such political fund-raising, "the mother's milk of politics," was no longer acceptable and was criminal. The Republicans said the president raised money at the White House with his coffee klatches and that it's unseemly to use the White House for such purposes. But we know that the White House has been used for these same purposes by Clinton's Republican predecessors. For example, videotapes show President Reagan in May 1984 and April 1985 seeking contributions from wealthy donors in the East Room of the White House. The fact that Clinton elevated this practice to an art doesn't make it any more improper or criminal.

But, the Republicans said, Clinton also raised money over the phone from the Oval Office in the White House, a crime. (And Vice President Gore did the same from his office.) The applicable statute—18 U.S.C. §607(a)—reads that it is "unlawful for any person to solicit or receive any contribution . . . in any [federal government] room or building *occupied in the discharge of official duties.*" That means there would be a *possible* violation if President Clinton made the calls from the Oval Office as opposed to the living quarters of the White House. I say "possible" because in 1979 the Office of Legal Counsel of the Justice Department said it isn't clear whether or not the statute only applies where *the person solicited* is on federal property at the time of the solicitation. Here, the phone calls were made to private donors who were not on any federal property. In fact, the nonpartisan Congressional Research Service reported in August 1997: "In more than one hundred years since its enactment [Sec. 607(a) has never been] applied in any prosecution to cover one who solicits a campaign contribution from a federal building by letter or telephone to persons who are not located themselves in a federal building." This is consistent with the legislative intent behind the statute (the Pendleton Act, which dates all the way back to 1883), which was to put an end to the practice of federal officials' shaking down their employees, on federal property during the workday, for campaign contributions. Moreover, since a 1980 amendment to Section 607, if the money raised is "soft" money, that is, for a political party and not for a specific candidate ("hard" money), it's *not* against the law.

On December 2, 1997, Attorney General Janet Reno announced that after an extensive investigation by "a task force of experienced attorneys and FBI agents" the Justice Department concluded that all of the money solicited by Clinton and Gore was "soft" money. Also, that "telephone records, White House operator diaries, and investigative interviews all established that [the president's] calls were made from the White House residence, not from the Oval Office . . ." But let's assume a falsity, that the president raised all of his money from the Oval Office rather than from the living quarters of the White House. If it's against the law, it's only a highly, highly technical violation that no one should have spent a moment's time on. As they say in the law, it's a "distinction without substance." Or, as scientists are fond of saying, a difference is a difference only if it makes a difference. I mean, it would be okay if the president had left the Oval Office and went to his private quarters at the White House to make the calls, or with his Secret Service detail gone across the street to a rented room to make the calls, but it's not okay if he made the calls from his office? Who cares where he made his calls? Actually, other than mostly the right wing of the Republican Party, hardly anyone *did* care. The whole affair was a nonevent that virtually no one followed. Yet the "liberal" media made this an enormous, banner story, plastering it on the front pages of newspapers day after day for months, like they would if someone had found a mutilated corpse in the White House basement.

Oh, by the way, the Republicans were aghast that a foreign government (China) may have tried to influence the last presidential election by contributing money to the Democratic Party, which is prohibited by law. But apart from the hypocrisy of this charge (in that many times, under both Democratic and Republican administrations, this country has with money, political know-how, and much more unsavory methods tried to influence foreign elections), again, the Republicans have done the same thing. For instance, it's been documented that Haley Barbour, the former Republican Party chairman, arranged for a $1.6 million contribution from a Hong Kong real estate company that ended up in the coffers of the Republican National Committee in the critical closing weeks of the 1994 congressional elections.

Although this supposed scandal was the driest reading in the world, I decided to force myself to go through page after page of the daily newspapers about all of these allegations for an entire week to see if I could find any evidence, any evidence at all, of the *only* thing that would have any significant relevance in this almost meaningless story: whether there was a quid pro quo, that is, whether in return for the money (from a foreign or domestic source) some favor was granted to the giver, either by executive order, legislation, or by some other means. If not, on a scale of one to ten, it's a negative one in importance. If there *was* a quid pro quo, it's a ten, inasmuch as that substitutes a private, special interest for the public interest, essentially negating our democratic, representational form of government. This criminal behavior (bribery), we all know, has been going on for years in America. "We've got the best Congress money can buy," Will Rogers once observed. And Senator John McCain (R-Ariz.) noted, "Special interests play a huge role in legislation; otherwise, these appropriation bills would not be larded with pork, and tax-code bills would not be loaded with loopholes."

That big business and special-interest groups have been financing federal, state, and even local elections for both parties in America for decades, and getting substantial benefits in return that are directly antithetical to the general public's interest and welfare, is too well known a fact even to be cataloged. For instance, if Republican support on Capitol Hill for big business and the NRA as well as Democratic support for labor unions and trial lawyers is unrelated to financial contributions from these groups, then Frenchmen don't drink wine. But I found no evidence in the vast reportage on the fund-raising "scandal" (at least in the particular week of papers I read) of an actual quid pro quo. In fact, the media focused just about all of its attention on the alleged contributions themselves, virtually ignoring the only issue that matters.

In some instances, foreign and/or domestic contributions to the Democrats may very well have influenced the Democrats—I mean, that's usually the reason for the campaign contribution—but without the evidence to prove it, the whole fund-raising "scandal" was a giant nonstory. Yet the "liberal" media could hardly have given the mere fact of the contributions, not the important issue of what, if anything, the giver received in return, more attention, and it was all against the Democratic president, his vice president, and the Democratic Party.[6]

Can one say, "Well, Clinton leaves something to be desired when it comes to morality, and this is why the press has been so hard on him"? No. President Carter, as clean as a hound's tooth and one of the most moral men ever to inhabit the Oval Office, was also continuously and mercilessly savaged by the media. Yet Reagan and Bush and their administrations, for the most part, received a free ride from the "liberal media."

In addition to Iran-Contra, another example of this free ride was Bush's supposed affair with his longtime secretary, which was circumstantially attested to by third parties, yet received virtually no coverage by the media in the 1992 presidential election. Yet another example took place in the 1988 presidential campaign between then–Vice President Bush and Michael Dukakis, during which evidence (which admittedly is not synonymous with proof) surfaced that the release of the fifty-two American hostages in Iran on January 20, 1981, the day of President Reagan's inauguration, may have been held up until after the 1980 election by their Iranian captors working in league with the Reagan-Bush campaign to hurt the candidacy of then-President Jimmy Carter, who had earlier unsuccessfully attempted to rescue the hostages. Allegedly, representatives of the Reagan-Bush campaign met with the Iranians in Madrid and Paris and promised the secret sale of arms to the Khomeini regime (which, we know, did in fact later take place) in return for delaying the release of the hostages. (The main go-between was thought to be William Casey, the Reagan-Bush campaign manager and later director of the CIA, a notoriously shadowy and secretive figure whose view of an effective clandestine operation was that if the participants said nothing at all they were talking too much.) This not only was an extremely serious allegation, but it was an obviously intriguing story, one worth exploring. The "liberal" media, however, essentially gave Reagan and Bush a pass on the matter, never vigorously pursuing the many leads and consigning most of its very infrequent coverage of the allegations to the inside pages. Put it this way: The media gave the Republican investigation of Democratic fund-raising practices fifty times as much attention. And that is not an exaggeration.

After three years of research and hundreds of interviews, Gary Sick, who served on the National Security Council staff under Presidents Ford, Carter, and Reagan, and participated in the negotiations over the release of the hostages, wrote in his 1991 book, *October Surprise: America's Hostages in Iran and the Election of Ronald Reagan,* that "the critical question is whether representatives of a political party out of power secretly, and illegally, negotiated with representatives of a hostile foreign power, thereby distorting or undermining the efforts of the legitimate government. Even today, more than a decade later, it is still difficult to imagine that an opposition political faction in the United States would employ such tactics, willfully prolonging the imprisonment of fifty-two American citizens for partisan political gain. Nevertheless, that is what occurred: the Reagan-Bush campaign mounted a professionally organized intelligence operation to subvert the American democratic process." Sick's conclusion may very well be wrong. (Indeed, although many, such as former AP and *Newsweek* reporter Robert Parry and veteran White House correspondent Sarah McClendon, have rejected the findings as being a superficial whitewash, separate Senate and House task force committees—no independent counsel was ever appointed—concluded in 1992 and 1993 that they were unable to find any "credible evidence" to support the allegations.) But one thing is clear. This was a sensational allegation that should have been a big media story for months. But it was not.

One may wonder why a mostly liberal media is so hard on Democrats and, conversely, soft on Republicans. I don't have the absolute answer to that question, but I can suggest some possible reasons. The media, well aware of the charge constantly leveled against them that they are "soft" on Democrats, may be unconsciously (or even consciously) trying to demonstrate to the right wing how fair and impartial they are. In the process, they overcompensate. Also, although most members of the media are Democrats, the wealthy owners of the big papers, television networks, and radio stations they work for are mostly Republicans, and consciously or subconsciously, they may be trying to please their bosses. And let's not forget that although the far left and the far right—which are actually closer to each other than they are to moderates in the middle, since they share a common denominator, fanaticism—are both batty, as a general rule the far right is more strident, persistent, and uncivilized. They therefore make more noise, make more charges, and hence give the media more to report on.

As previously indicated, it's perfectly normal to assume and expect the Supreme Court, the highest court in the land, to know what the law is. I mean, if they don't, who does? The high court as an institution occupies a position of enormous stature, probity, and respect in our society. As a *Los Angeles Daily News* editorial on July 6, 1997, put it: "When the U.S. Supreme Court speaks, the American public still listens. That nine people still have the ability to decide the fate of a nation and that a nation respects and abides by those decisions, is one of the greatest testaments standing today to the wisdom and power of the U.S. Constitution."

The Court evokes, then, a sense of order, dignity, and incorruptibility possessed by no other entity, public or private, in America. Indeed, the Court, by its legal rulings, has kept this nation on an ethical and moral course through the roiling currents and vicissitudes of wars, depressions, and civil conflicts.

But there's another reality. The Court, after all, consists of nine very *human* beings whose black robes do not miraculously imbue them with, or divest them of, strengths or weaknesses they did not possess before being sworn in as justices. And their rulings are not as changeless as truth. The law is, at any moment in time, substantially dependent upon the legal and oftentimes political ideology of the judges who interpret it. Presidents, who appoint Supreme Court justices, know this, of course. That's why they almost always appoint people to the Court who they believe by and large share their political and social philosophies. Some presidents (most notably Lincoln between 1861 and 1864 and FDR in 1937) literally tried to "pack" the Court with justices they felt would be supportive of their agenda. (Sometimes this tactic backfires. President Eisenhower said that "the biggest damned-fool mistake I ever made" was appointing Earl Warren, supposedly a law-and-order Republican, to be chief justice. The Warren Court turned out to be perhaps the most liberal Supreme Court ever.) Most Supreme Court justices, though qualified, are on the bench in large part because of their political background. And this is true, unfortunately, even with the chief justices. For instance, the last three chief justices of the U.S. Supreme Court have been creatures of politics. Earl Warren was the chairman and keynote speaker at the Republican National Convention in 1944 and the vice presidential nominee on the Republican ticket in 1948. Warren Burger in 1948 was the floor manager for Minnesota governor Harold Stassen's home-state candidacy at the Republican National Convention, and in 1952 he pledged the Minnesota delegation to Dwight Eisenhower's presidential bid at the convention. (With no previous judicial experience at all, in 1956 Burger was appointed by Eisenhower to the U.S. Court of Appeals.) Talk about the political vineyards, William Rehnquist (an active political supporter of Barry Goldwater's 1964 bid for the presidency) provided on-site legal advice in 1962 to Republicans assigned the task of challenging voters' credentials at a Phoenix polling location. The charge by witnesses that he had intimidated black and Hispanic voters on the ground of their inability to read was denied by Rehnquist.

One of the most blatantly political appointments to the Supreme Court in recent memory was that of Clarence Thomas in 1991 to replace Thurgood Marshall. Though he was only forty-two, had never distinguished himself as a lawyer or on the bench (just one year on the U.S. Court of Appeals), and was not rated "highly qualified" by the American Bar Association, he apparently was what President Bush was looking for at the time—a very conservative black. Remarkably, during his Senate confirmation hearing Thomas testified that he had never once debated with anyone the merits of *Roe v. Wade*, the landmark Supreme Court decision on abortion. He has since lived up to his meager reputation, becoming a profoundly intellectual mynah bird, without his own independent voice, of Justice Antonin Scalia.

Over time, the law applicable to a given set of facts can be as varied and different as the intellect and leanings of the justices seated on the bench—the Court not infrequently overruling a decision made by prior justices.[7] As Justice Scalia wryly observed in *South Carolina v. Gathers*, 490 U.S. 805 (1989): "Overrulings of precedent rarely occur without a change in the Court's personnel." Stare decisis, the policy of courts to stand by precedent and not disturb that which has been established in prior decisions, is only a policy, not a binding rule, and is frequently ignored with very deft but nonetheless transparent legal gymnastics. There's perhaps no clearer evidence that the law is not an absolute, that it is not something whose essence everyone can see and firmly grasp, than the fact that the Supreme Court justices routinely cannot agree among themselves as to what the law *is*. Every time the Court rules, for instance, five-four or six-three, a very common occurrence, that's saying that five or six justices believe the law with respect to a given situation is one thing, and the other three or four believe it is something else.

It should be noted that although the justices, being ordinary human beings, are capable of the same irrationality to which we all at times succumb, the Court has nine members, and the phrase "saner counsel will prevail" has, for the most part, characterized the rulings of the Court; that is, when any position of one or more members of the Court has been outlandish or bizarre, it's been safely tucked away as a dissent at the tail end of the majority opinion.

But in the Paula Jones case, as we shall see, saner counsel did not prevail.

The second prefatory matter I want to discuss is the downright crazy and even alien (at least to me) direction in which our modern society seems to be inexorably proceeding—a direction that causes me to wonder if we, as a people, are losing our marbles. It causes me to wonder where, if at all, there remains in our society an island of sanity, anchored securely in common sense, reason, and tradition, an island amidst the constant, everyday assaults upon our sensibilities. If that island is not the U.S. Supreme Court—the highest court in the land, consisting of nine mature, educated, and experienced men and women with presumably impeccable characters and backgrounds, who essentially have lifetime appointments (Art. 3, §1 of the United States Constitution: "shall hold their Offices *during good Behavior*") so as to make them immune from self-preservation and partisan pressures—then to whom can we look? If you can't find a sanctuary of common sense in the U.S. Supreme Court, where can you go? (Since one tends to equate, to a certain degree, common sense with the notion of justice, was Supreme Court Justice Oliver Wendell Holmes telling us something in this regard years ago when he said to a young whippersnapper lawyer who injected the word *justice* one too many times into his oral argument before the court: "I must remind you, young man, this is a court of law, not a court of justice"?) It's somewhat remindful to me of a murder case I tried years ago in which a San Diego husband and wife, wanting to get away from a big-city life that was becoming increasingly unsafe, went to a peaceful, idyllic, uninhabited South Sea isle, where they were brutally murdered and left at the bottom of the island's lagoon. A worse end than could have ever happened to them in San Diego.

We live in a society that has gone from the Lincoln-Douglas debates to campaigns for the presidency—where the very destiny of this nation is at stake—being conducted by sound bites. What better example of the insanity in our society than the O.J. Simpson murder case? From the very beginning, the Simpson case, though a sensational murder, received a vastly disproportionate amount of publicity. Unbelievably, all three networks in America covered Simpson's entire preliminary hearing live. *Newsweek,* which did an incredible *seven* cover stories on the case, devoted almost its entire October 16, 1995, edition to the Simpson trial verdict. On the same week of the Simpson verdict, Hurricane Opal tore through Florida and neighboring states. More than a hundred thousand people were left homeless, much of a 140-mile stretch between Mobile, Alabama, and Panama City, Florida, was demolished, and eighteen people died. Yet Opal's devastation warranted only one paragraph in *News-week*'s Periscope section, and even then, there was not one single word on the damage that the hurricane had wrought. The paragraph dealt exclusively with Dan Rather's reporting on the hurricane, and a photograph showed him clinging to a pole in the wind. *Newsweek* added, "Rather nabbed what some [certainly not *Newsweek*] would argue was the real story of the week."

The electronic media were even more excessive in their coverage, if possible, than the print media. Even though the trial was already being covered in its entirety by Court TV and other cable outlets, CNN also provided gavel-to-gavel coverage, thereby telling its audience day in and day out for over nine months, in their opinion this was the most important news story in the entire world. And *Larry King Live*, the principal talk show on CNN in the evening, dealt far, far more with the Simpson case than with any other news event. King told his viewers, "If we had God booked, and O.J. was available, we'd move God."

The television networks weren't much better. From the time of the murders to the end of the trial, CBS, NBC, and ABC, in addition to doing a great number of specials, had thirty-eight hours and fifty-four minutes of news coverage on the case. During that same period, only four hours and fourteen minutes were devoted to the entire debate over national health care. Even the previously serious-minded *Nightline* had an outlandish fifty-nine segments on the case over an eighteen-month period. I suppose all this means that the Simpson case was a story for the ages, one that was considerably more important than such mundane events as the fall of Communism, the drug crisis, and presidential elections.

We're so upside-down in our society that we make heroes out of those who aren't, such as John Wayne, a patriotic, red-blooded, two-fisted American who spent the Second World War in the trenches on the movie lots of Hollywood. In our passion for heroes, we have bastardized the meaning of the word beyond recognition. To me, the word *hero* has always implied courage, and courage, in turn, implies a choice. When the young American fighter pilot Scott O'Grady was shot down over Bosnian Serb territory in June of 1996 and hid in a Bosnian forest for six days until he was rescued (at one point lying motionless on the ground between the legs of a cow that was feeding on blades of grass), under what conceivable definition does this fine young man's effort to survive qualify as the conduct of a hero? Yet he was treated like one by this country and even feted by the president at the White House.

When Captain O'Grady himself, eschewing the hero status he had suddenly achieved, told a gaggle of reporters that "all I was, was a scared little bunny rabbit, trying to survive," the media would have none of it. What did the pilot know? We know a hero when we see one, they said to themselves. "An American hero came home to an emotional Main Street welcome," the *Los Angeles Times* and other newspapers gushed. "He is an American hero," President Clinton proclaimed. *Time, Newsweek,* and *U.S. News & World Report* all had cover stories on the incident. "One Amazing Kid" and "The Right Stuff," *U.S. News* and *Newsweek* trumpeted on their covers.

But a hero, I always thought, was someone who had risked his or her life to help another. The four American helicopter pilots and their crews who flew into enemy territory and withstood deadly enemy ground fire to rescue O'Grady were the *real* heroes in this piece, but hardly a word was said about them.

Our desperate search for heroes is so intense that Mills Lane, the referee in the June 28, 1997, Mike Tyson–Evander Holyfield heavy-weight championship fight who disqualified Tyson in the third round after Tyson, who gave new meaning to the term "hungry fighter," actually bit off a chunk of Holyfield's right ear (Tyson had bitten Holyfield's left ear less than a minute earlier, causing Holyfield to leap in pain across the ring), has also been lauded and treated like a hero by many. "He's a hero," the sports editor of the *Los Angeles Times* proclaimed. There were tributes to Lane around the country. Jay Leno, *Larry King Live, Good Morning America,* and just about everyone else wanted him on their shows. "It's beyond my wildest dreams what has happened to me since the Holyfield fight," Lane said. He was the "Cover Story" in *USA Today,* the paper saying that Lane "has been universally praised" for his performance in the fight. But why? Although Lane is a fine referee, not only didn't he do any-thing "heroic," but wasn't he just doing what any rational referee would have done under the circumstances? Are we to believe that other referees would have waited until Tyson approached Holyfield with a jar of mustard and ketchup before finally stepping in? How crazy can we get?

There are countless examples of the insanity and topsy-turvy direction in which our society is going. These are but a very few (only symbolic of the craziness and decline in our society, and in no particular categories or order of importance) that quickly come to mind. There are very few things more important to the culture and soul of a nation than its music. Yet predominantly, our younger generation no longer listens to music, which, definitionally, has a melody, but to rap—someone *talking* accompanied by a beat. And girls today wear rings not only on their ears and fingers, but unbelievably on their nose and tongue, even their navel.

There are metal detectors for knives and guns at many high schools, even some *junior* high schools.

A good spanking when a child deserved it used to be considered a normal part of a child's discipline. But today's parent administering a spanking has to risk being accused of child abuse and prosecuted as a criminal.

The three-minute "trailers" for movies today are usually three minutes of one loud explosion after another. And now Hollywood has decided to offend us—in addition to the obligatory and gratuitous sex in virtually every film, whether a part of the plot or not—by showing us people going to the bathroom. Yes—you heard me right. Incredibly, some of these crass, "artistic" people, right in the middle of their movies, have decided to show men not just standing at urinals, but men and women sitting on toilets, something, of course, we all want to see very badly.

Street gangs used to fight each other with their fists and with clubs; today they kill complete strangers, including children and pregnant women, in drive-by shootings.

Even our gender identity has become blurred. Men today also wear earrings (and even nose rings). Bone-thin models, young girls who look like starving young boys, are promoted as the epitome of sexuality; a healthy-looking woman with a curvaceous figure is now seen as *undesirable*. In years gone by, teenage girls all used to wear skirts, which are distinctly feminine attire, to school and elsewhere.

Today, it's almost impossible to find any who do. They almost all wear blue jeans, which are distinctly male attire.

In the same vein, we read today where women are lifting heavy weights, even boxing. In fact, we're becoming such an androgynous society that the voices of several young male singers today are such that frequently one can't tell from a recording if it's a man or a woman singing.

A woman's role used to be in the home, cooking and taking care of the children. The man worked outside the home and was the breadwinner. But in our topsy-turvy world today, most women don't want to stay at home anymore. They think it's demeaning. But my view is that unless it's not economically feasible, a woman's role, at least up until the time the children go to school, should normally be in the home. The reason really is almost too obvious to state. If she's not supposed to be at home taking care of the children, who is? Is it more natural for the man to assume this role? Or should the children grow up not being nurtured by their mother, but by a stranger being brought into the home to do so? Why so many women feel that being at home is a subordinate or secondary role to working outside the home, I haven't the faintest idea. It's just as challenging and important a role as that of being the breadwinner. Obviously, *someone* has to fill this role, and it's a far more natural role for the mother. But not in the crazy world we now live in. In the beginning, women felt there was a certain cachet about having a career outside the home. Today, it's become de rigueur. (Incidentally, to demonstrate that I am not antediluvian in my social and cultural views, if a woman does choose a career outside the home, I feel she should be treated 100 percent equally with men in pay and every other way that her abilities warrant.)

I don't condemn anyone for their lifestyle, as long as it doesn't impinge on the rights of others, and if this is the way husbands and wives want to live, that's certainly fine with me. And whether their particular familial arrangement is good or bad from a societal view-point is admittedly open to question. But I'll tell you what isn't open to question. It may only be a coincidence, and many other variables and imponderables may be contributing factors, but in the days when mothers were at home taking care of their children, we had far, far less crime in America, children had far more respect for their parents and authority, and there were far, far fewer divorces. Oh, by the way. There were also a lot fewer psychiatrists in those days, and the ones there were weren't nearly as well-off as they are today.

Perhaps serving as the best metaphor for the alarming decline in our society (massive foreign takeovers of our corporations and institutions by countries whom we defeated on the battlefield in the Second World War; by far the highest crime rate of any modern industrialized society; the shameful, lowering quality of our children's education, and so forth), is that buildings constructed today, using modern technology that earlier generations couldn't even fantasize about, aren't nearly as sturdy, aesthetic, or even architecturally inspired as those in the past.

We can't find sanity today even in sports. How many readers have heard of Kevin Garnett? One out of twenty? Well, Kevin averaged seventeen points and eight rebounds last year for the NBA Minneapolis Timberwolves, a good but hardly extraordinary season. Anyway, Kevin, just one year out of high school, *rejected* a six-year, $103 million offer from the Timberwolves this past summer. *$103 million!* But I didn't blame Kevin; after all, a man has to think of his future. In October, Kevin finally agreed to sign for $126 million. "It's not about money," Kevin said. I can imagine. If it were, I'm sure Kevin would have asked for a hell of a lot more.

While we're talking about basketball, what type of madness (and this is true of all major sports today, as opposed to when we were a more levelheaded nation) is it to play an incredibly grueling five-month season, with injuries, disputes, screaming fans, nail-biting games, and then, when it is all over, have a situation where, as Michael Jordan put it, "Now the *real* season begins"? You play eighty-two games just to get the home-court advantage in one more game (out of five or seven) than your opponent? So that a team like Seattle in the 1994–95 season can prove to be the best team during the regular season (when a great many more games are played, and hence, is the best indicator by far of which team is the best), but for whatever reason, including unfortunate injuries to key players, loses in the first round of the playoffs and their regular season becomes meaningless. What in the blessed hell was the eighty-two-game season for? Were they just essentially exhibition games? The 1997 World Series is just another example. Atlanta, a National League division champ and the majors' winningest team during the 162-game regular season, lost to the eventual World Series champion Florida Marlins, a wild-card team, in the second round of the playoffs. The Marlins beat the other National League division champ, San Francisco, in the first round. The Marlins' opposition, the Cleveland Indians, got to the World Series over three other major-league teams that had better records during the regular season. During this World Series matchup, Marlins manager Jim Leyland said, "The teams that played best *when they had to* are here." Right. They didn't *have* to win more than the other teams (that were in the playoffs) during the regular season because those were just exhibition games, right? It's crazy, yet the owners, out of sheer greed, are permitted to get by with this insanity of a "second season" (which, I repeat, we never used to have) because the fans don't seem to be troubled by it at all.

I could go on and on. Other than freedom of speech, nothing is more cherished or sacred in America than our right to privacy. But as *Time* said in its August 25, 1997, edition: "[We] have no secrets [anymore]. At the ATM window, on the Internet, even walking down the street, people are watching [our] every move."

I think we all know that today when you call a business or office you rarely have a human being answer the phone. It's normally a recorded voice giving you a menu of seven or eight selections to choose from. Thinking that surely the number you push will allow you to finally speak to someone who is breathing and can talk to you, you frequently have just begun. There are another five or six possibilities to choose from. Not infrequently this insanity goes on for several exasperating minutes before a live voice comes on the line. This, of course, is bad enough as it is. But are you aware that some major companies in America are so screwed up that they've now taken this madness to a new level? That unless you already know the extension or specific name of a person at the company you want to talk to, or one you think might be able to help you, no live voice will *ever* come on the line? That you literally cannot *ever* get past a recorded voice to an operator who can help you?

Things are getting so upside down in our society that you can't even *compliment* some people anymore. Take blacks. Anyone who knows me will tell you I don't have a racist bone in my body, but if you compliment blacks, to many of them this means you're saying they're somehow different than whites, so it then becomes an *insult*. For instance, although blacks are only 12 percent of our population, NBA starting fives are almost all black today, sprinters in track are almost all black, and when is the last time anyone has ever seen a white running back in pro football, even college ball? Without exception, every player who is a star, breakaway runner is black. I once asked the Cleveland Browns' all-time football great Jim Brown, considered by many to be the greatest running back ever, who was the last great white running back—not the big, hulking, battering-ram fullbacks who crash the middle of the line for a needed yard or two, but the swift, open-field, long-gain runner. After a few moments' pause, he answered: "Hugh McElhenny," a halfback for the 49ers, Vikings, and Giants. For the reader's information, McElhenny's playing years were from 1952 to 1964, *several decades ago*. For whatever reason, blacks obviously are superior athletes to whites. Why else do you think you look out on an NBA game and often see ten blacks and no whites? Because they look better in their uniforms than whites do? Yet when that poor devil Jimmy the Greek, who had always been a very good friend to black athletes and contributed to black causes, pointed out a few years ago that blacks were superior athletes and tried to hypothesize why, his politically correct superiors kicked his rear end out of his office at CBS so fast he didn't even have time to turn off the lights.

Talk about everything being upside down in our society, listen to this. The Americans with Disabilities Act was passed in 1990 to combat discrimination in the workplace against people with physical and mental disabilities. However, certain people are not protected by the act; for example, those currently engaging in the illegal use of drugs, kleptomaniacs, pyromaniacs, pedophiles, and so forth. What about those with "antisocial personality disorders"? According to guidelines promulgated on March 25, 1997, by the Equal Employment Opportunity Commission (which was established by the Disabilities Act to issue guidelines and regulations to enforce the act's provisions), these people cannot be discriminated against. Who, precisely, are these people? The EEOC refers us to the American Psychiatric Association's *Diagnostic and Statistical Manual of Mental Disorders* for a definition. When one goes to the manual, one sees these are people whose "disorder" is characterized by "repeatedly performing acts that are grounds for arrest . . . repeated lying, use of aliases or conning others for personal profit or pleasure . . . irritability and aggressiveness as indicated by repeated physical fights or assaults, reckless disregard for safety of self or others, consistent irresponsibility as indicated by repeated failure to sustain consistent work behavior or honor financial obligations"—in other words, what we used to call sociopaths.

In the old days, you'd simply fire these people, right? Not anymore. Not only can't they be fired, they don't even have to change or make any effort to adjust to the workplace. *The workplace has to adjust to them.* Unbelievably, the pathetically permissive idiots at the EEOC feel that these people have a "personality disorder" that is a protectible disability, and the EEOC says that "an employer must [now] provide a reasonable accommodation" to them, unless the employer can show "that the accommodation would impose" not just any hardship, but an "undue" hardship. So what does an employer, seeing it has such a person in its employ, have to do? Wait until the sociopath comes in one morning with a semiautomatic rifle and blows everyone away? Or until he's holding your ankles as you hang from a fifty-third-story window and is telling you that unless you promise never to speak to him in a cross manner again, he's going to let go?

Today, America is far more litigious than it has ever been, the most sue-happy nation in the entire world. No other nation even comes close to us. For instance, a recent study showed that the United States had about ten times as many tort actions (automobile collisions, assault and battery, libel and slander, and so forth) per capita as Britain, thirty-five times as many malpractice suits, and nearly one hundred times as many product-liability lawsuits.

As if that's not bad enough, Americans today are filing absolutely insane lawsuits that were virtually unheard of in earlier years. Just a few among hundreds of examples: A San Francisco woman sued the city's municipal railway for $500,000, claiming a cable car accident had turned her into a nymphomaniac. Remarkably, in the case known as the "Cable Car Named Desire," a jury awarded her

$50,000. A former student sued Gonzaga University for $110,000 after its law school flunked her out, alleging that her college grades should have alerted the university that she wouldn't do well in law school and that they should therefore have rejected her application for admission. A New York State prison inmate sued the state for the prison's refusal to provide a salad bar. In Florida, a burglar on the roof of a home in the middle of the night, trying to find a way to get in, fell through a skylight, sustaining multiple injuries. He sued the homeowners for his injuries, claiming the skylight was defective, and won the lawsuit.

I saw a cartoon a few days ago where a police officer is shown arresting a suspect and the suspect proceeds to advise the officer of the officer's constitutional rights.

There are so many other examples of madness in our society. But enough.

In a crazy society that is only getting progressively worse, and with the light at the end of the tunnel being an oncoming train, one would like to think that the U.S. Supreme Court, the highest court in the land, is the one island of sanity still remaining. But if what you folks are about to read is any indication, we've all got a lot to worry about. The question that presents itself is whether the near-pathological dizziness and irrationality in our society has so invaded this nation's marrow that, like a wildly infectious virus, even the Supreme Court is not immune.

PART TWO

The U.S. Supreme Court Decision
in the Case of
Paula Corbin Jones v. William Jefferson Clinton

THE ALLEGED FACTS and legal history that led up to the Supreme Court decision in Paula Jones's lawsuit against the president are these:

On May 6, 1994, Paula Jones filed a complaint, #LR-C-94-290, in the U.S. District Court for the Eastern District of Arkansas against President Clinton (as well as against Danny Ferguson, a former Arkansas state-police officer who was assigned to Clinton's security detail). She alleged in her complaint that on May 8, 1991, Clinton, then governor of the state of Arkansas, delivered a speech at the third annual Governor's Quality Management Conference at the Excelsior Hotel in Little Rock. During the conference, Jones, an employee for the Arkansas Industrial Development Commission (AIDC), a state agency, worked at the registration desk with another AIDC employee. She says that at approximately 2:30 P.M. that day, which was after Clinton's speech, Ferguson appeared at the registration desk, handed her a piece of paper with a suite number at the Excelsior on it, and told her "the governor would like to meet with you" in the suite. Thinking it would be an honor to meet the governor and that it would perhaps lead to an enhanced employment opportunity, she proceeded to the room escorted by Ferguson, who remained outside. She says the president "shook [her] hand, invited her in, and closed the door." She alleges that "after a few minutes of small talk with Clinton," he took her hand and pulled her toward him. She removed her hand and retreated, whereupon Clinton approached her again, saying, "I love the way your hair flows down your back" and "I love your curves." While saying these things, he put his hand on her leg and "started sliding it toward the hem of [her] culottes" and also "bent down to attempt to kiss" her on the neck. Jones says that she exclaimed to the president, "What are you doing?" and "escaped from Clinton's physical proximity by walking away." She alleges she then took a seat at the end of a sofa. Clinton asked if she was married, and when she replied she was not but had a boyfriend, he sat down next to her on the sofa, "lowered his trousers and underwear exposing his erect penis," and asked her to "kiss it." She alleges she became "horrified, jumped up from the couch," and told him she wasn't "that kind of girl," adding, "Look, I've got to go." Clinton replied, "Well, I don't want to make you do anything you don't want to do" and told her if she got into any trouble for leaving her desk to "have Dave [whom she took to mean Dave Harrington, her boss] call me immediately and I'll take care of it." As she left the room, she alleges, Clinton looked sternly at her and said, "You are smart. Let's keep this between ourselves." She said she was "visibly shaken and upset" and returned to the registration desk, where she told her coworker, Pamela Blackard, everything that had happened. She alleges further that she and a friend, Debra Ballentine, were dining at the Golden Corral steakhouse in Little Rock on January 8, 1994, when they saw Ferguson and his wife at a nearby table. Ferguson, she says, came to their table and, among other things, told her, "Clinton told me you wouldn't do anything [in the room], Paula."

Jones's complaint seeks $175,000 for each of the four counts of the complaint—$75,000 in actual damages and $100,000 in punitive damages. The most important count, and the heart of the lawsuit, is count one, which alleges a civil rights violation by Clinton against Jones under 42 U.S.C. §1983,[8] in that "Clinton, as Governor of Arkansas, under color of state law, discriminated against [her] because of her gender by sexually harassing and assaulting her," thereby depriving her "of her right to equal protection of the law" under the Fourteenth Amendment to the United States Constitution. (Count two alleges a conspiracy between the president and Ferguson to violate her civil rights; count three is for intentional infliction of emotional distress by Clinton against Jones; count four was for defamation against her by Clinton and Ferguson but was dismissed by the trial judge against the president on August 22, 1997. In an amended complaint filed by Jones on December 8, 1997, this count was deleted also as to Ferguson. Thus, the potential monetary damages against the president have been reduced from $700,000 to $525,000.)

Jones, twenty-four years old at the time of the alleged incident and earning $6.35 an hour, contends further in her complaint that after her encounter with Clinton she "was treated in a hostile and rude manner by certain superiors at AIDC" and was eventually "transferred to a position which had no responsible duties for which [she] could be adequately evaluated to earn advancement." She claims that "although other employees received merit increases, [she] never received a raise beyond a cost of living increase." She alleges these things were done because "she was being punished for [her] rejection of the . . . advances made by Clinton." In a September 22, 1997, answer to an interrogatory submitted to her by the president's lawyers, Jones elaborated on the adversities she alleges befell her for resisting Clinton's sexual advances. "I was ostracized," she asserts, "by the people with whom I worked in purely emotional ways—for example, during my second year at AIDC I was singled out on Secretaries Day as the only person at my level not given flowers." (She acknowledges, however, by another answer to an interrogatory, that having trouble at the workplace is not uncommon for her. She says she was fired from four of five previous full-time jobs.) Outside the workplace, she claims that "private details of my life were investigated, by persons whose names I do not know, and the information thus gathered was displayed to me in a manner that was intended to frighten me, and that did frighten me: it suggested that I was being watched and/or followed, by law enforcement personnel, at then-Governor Clinton's request, because Mr. Clinton wanted to engage in sex with me and as a way of inducing me to engage in sex with him, or as a way of punishing me because I refused to do so."

In a separate, cryptic paragraph devoid of details or background, Jones alleges in the above answer to the interrogatory that "I was physically touched by Mr. Clinton after May 8, 1991, and at the time of this second touching Mr. Clinton falsely claimed to certain persons that he and I were 'a couple.' "

Jones terminated her employment at AIDC on February 20, 1993. By then married and with a child, she, her husband, and their child moved to California on May 4, 1993. Her suit, commonly referred to as an employment-based sexual harassment matter, was not filed under Title VII of the 1964 Civil Rights Act, which prohibits sexual harassment in the workplace, because that federal law's six-month statute of limitations had already run out at the time Jones filed her lawsuit. Her Section 1983 lawsuit has a three-year statute of limitations, and she filed it just *two days* before the statute of limitations for that section had run out.

The president, alleging temporary immunity from civil lawsuits during the term of his presidency, filed a motion on August 10, 1994, asking the district court in Little Rock to dismiss the complaint "without prejudice" to Jones, thereby allowing her to refile her complaint at the termination of his presidency, or, alternatively, to stay (suspend) the proceedings against him until the end of his term. The district court, on December 28, 1994, denied the president's motion to dismiss but stayed the trial until the end of his presidency. However, the court ruled that the discovery and deposition process could proceed *during* his term in office. Both parties appealed the court's ruling to the U.S. Court of Appeals, Eighth Circuit, in St. Louis. On January 9, 1996, the court of appeals reversed the lower court's ruling that the trial be postponed until the end of the president's term in office. The president then filed a petition for certiorari (an appeal) with the U.S. Supreme Court, seeking a reversal of the court of appeals' ruling.[9] On May 27, 1997, the Supreme Court affirmed the judgment of the court of appeals.

On July 3, 1997, the president filed an answer to the complaint in Little Rock, denying all of "the false allegations advanced in the complaint." The answer asserts that "at no time did the President make sexual advances toward the plaintiff, or otherwise act improperly in her presence." The answer goes on to say that although it was the president's practice, when he was governor, to have a business suite available at hotels for the purpose of making calls and receiving visitors, he "does not recall ever meeting" Paula Jones.

In codefendant Danny Ferguson's much earlier answer to the complaint, on January 10, 1994, he concedes that he took Paula Jones to the governor's room in the hotel but alleges that the genesis of their meeting was Paula Jones's telling him on the morning of the conference that "she found Governor Clinton to be 'good-looking' and about how she thought his hair was sexy, and which comments she asked [him] to relate to Governor Bill Clinton." He further alleges that after she emerged from the governor's room some twenty to thirty minutes after having been left there by him, she asked him if he and the governor were going to stay at the seminar for the rest of the day. When he replied it was up to the governor, he says she then asked "if the Governor had a girlfriend" and when he replied that Clinton did not, "she then responded that she would be the Governor's girlfriend. Plaintiff, Paula Jones, did not appear to be upset in any way." He further alleges that approximately "a week or two after the aforesaid conference, Plaintiff Paula Jones came into the Governor's office to deliver mail." When she saw him she asked if the governor had said anything to him about her. He replied that Clinton had not, and "Plaintiff Paula Corbin Jones then asked for a piece of paper and a pen and wrote down her home phone number and told [me] to give it to the Governor. She said to tell him that she was living with her boyfriend and that if the boyfriend answered, Governor Clinton should either hang up or say that he had a wrong number." Ferguson denies, in his answer to the complaint, Jones's rendition of the January 8, 1994, steakhouse conversation in Little Rock, recalling instead that Jones asked him "how much money [Ferguson] thought that she could make for herself by coming forward with her allegations."

The issue before the Supreme Court was whether or not a sitting president could be forced to go to trial during his term of office to defend himself in a civil (not criminal) action arising out of alleged misconduct unrelated to his official presidential duties. The president (through his lawyers) argued that the Constitution required the federal courts to defer any litigation against a sitting president, related or unrelated to his duties, until his term ends. So, contrary to much misconception among the American public, the president was not claiming to be "above the law," that is, immune from civil process. Even the Supreme Court, in its otherwise deplorable decision, acknowledged the fact that "petitioner [the president] . . . does not contend that the occupant of the Office of the President is 'above the law' in the sense that his conduct is entirely immune from judicial scrutiny. The President argues merely for a postponement of the judicial proceedings." The issue was not *whether* Paula Jones should be able to have her day in court, but *when*.

In reaching their decision, there was pressure on the Court to rule against the president. The Court had to know that the nation's media were for the most part emphatically against the president's position. Why? Because of the media's incompetence, the president's simple request for a postponement had metamorphosed into his wanting to be "above the law." The real question had become whether or not he was, and the resounding answer one heard almost everywhere in the media was that he was not. "No citizen—not even a sitting President—is above the law," declared the lead editorial in the January 13, 1997, *New York Times*, urging the Court to deny the president's request for a postponement of the lawsuit. That no one was above the law, the *Times* editorial board assured its readers, was a "bedrock constitutional principle." "The President is not above the law," the *Washington Post* had said a year earlier in a January 10, 1996, editorial.

How a request for a continuance translates into being "above the law" (in other words, *absolute* immunity), one would have to ask the learned gentlemen on the editorial boards of these presumably knowledgeable newspapers. I personally cannot force a connection in my mind between the two.

The Court, consisting of nine sentient human beings, may possibly have been influenced, even if subliminally, by the positions taken in these two powerful papers. The Court likewise had to be aware that the mood of the nation's people, as reflected by surveys, was clear and unmistakable. The president was no different than they were. Hadn't they heard something dating from ancient England about even the king being "under God and the law"? Yeah. Right on. We're all equal. Who the heck does the president think he is, after all? "No one is above the law, Vince, not even the president," the owner of the station where I buy my gasoline assured me. A *CBS News/New York Times* national poll conducted between January 14 and 17, 1997, by the Roper Center for Public Opinion showed that 68 percent thought the case should proceed to trial during the president's term in office. Only 25 percent thought it should be continued. Seven percent had no opinion.

Of course, it's one thing for the citizen on the street, who is neither educated in nor overly concerned with the nuances of the law and constitutional niceties, to resolve these issues in his or her mind with clichéd, incorrect thinking.[10] But when the editorial boards of the nation's two most respected and influential daily newspapers, whose job it is to know whereof they speak, resort to simplistic and platitudinous reasoning, I, for one, find it offensive. After all, these are people who, every day of the year, pontificate like Delphic oracles in telling everyone, from the president, Congress, and the Supreme Court on down, what should and should not be done in our society. (Much more on these two papers later.)

Not only was the media, as we shall see, way off base when they suggested that the president's position required a finding that he was "above the law," but in a very real sense, while no one is above the law in all situations, thousands of people in our society *are*, in fact, literally "above the law" in many situations. Foreign diplomats in this country, under the 1961 Vienna Convention on Diplomatic Relations, enjoy absolute immunity, not just from most civil liability, but even from criminal process. Much less widely known is the fact that legislators, prosecutors, and judges (including members of the Supreme Court) enjoy *absolute* immunity from all civil lawsuits arising out of their official duties, *even when it is clear they have acted corruptly and maliciously.* (It should be noted that our legal ancestors, the British, by statute [Crown Proceedings Act, 1947, 10 & 11 Geo. 6, Cap. 44, Sec. 40(1)] prohibit all "proceedings in tort [a civil wrong] to be brought against His Majesty in His private capacity," apparently a latter-day remnant of the old English common law maxim "The king can do no wrong.")

In denying the president's request for a postponement of the trial as well as pretrial discovery and depositions, the Supreme Court, in an opinion written by Justice Stevens and joined in by seven other justices (Justice Breyer wrote a separate, concurring opinion), began by dicussing the absolute-immunity question, which they acknowledged the president wasn't even claiming in this case. The Court said that although presidents had absolute immunity from civil lawsuits predicated on their official acts—the rationale being that the lack of such immunity would render the president "unduly cautious in the discharge of his official duties"—this reasoning, they said, would clearly not be present where, as here, the president was being sued for his *un*official conduct; conduct, in fact, that allegedly took place before Clinton became president, when he was governor of Arkansas.

When the Court got down to the central issue before them—whether the president was entitled to a postponement of the civil suit—it began its inquiry thusly: "As a starting premise, petitioner [President Clinton] contends that he occupies a unique office with powers and responsibilities so vast and important that the public interest demands that he devote his undivided time and attention to his public duties. . . . We have no dispute with the initial premise of the argument. Former Presidents, from George Washington to George Bush, have consistently endorsed petitioner's characterization of the office."

Where the Court had problems was with the second prong of the argument made by the president's lawyers (hereinafter Bennett, for Robert S. Bennett, the president's main lawyer) that, given the nature of the office, the constitutional doctrine of separation of powers flowing from the three branches of government* placed limits on the *judicial* branch of government (here, the federal district court in Little Rock, where the case would be tried) interfering with the *executive* branch, limits that would be transgressed by allowing the action to proceed during the president's term in office. In Bennett's legal brief to the Court in support of his motion to stay the proceed-

---

*Article 1 of the United States Constitution sets forth the powers of the legislative branch (Congress) of government; Article 2, the powers of the executive branch (office of the presidency); Article 3, the powers of the judicial branch (the "Supreme Court, and . . . such inferior courts as the Congress may from time to time ordain and establish").

ings against the president, he took issue with the court of appeals' position that separation-of-powers problems could be avoided throughout the litigation because the president, the court of appeals said, could "pursue motions for rescheduling, additional time, or continuances" if he could show that the proceedings "interfer[ed] with specific, particularized, clearly articulated Presidential duties."

Under this approach, Bennett argued in his brief,

> The President would have to provide detailed information about the nature of pending Executive Branch matters requiring his attention, and the trial judge would have to pass judgment on the President's priorities. . . . Such a state of affairs is an extraordinary affront to the separation of powers. A trial judge—state or federal—would be examining the official priorities of the individual in whom the whole of the "Executive Power" is vested. And the judge would be not merely reviewing the President's priorities [on a day-to-day basis] but conceivably could order the President to rearrange them. The nature of the President's responsibilities makes it especially inappropriate for the Courts to insist on answers to the kinds of questions that inevitably would be posed under this regime. In situations involving matters of national security, sensitive diplomatic issues, or confidential intelligence or law enforcement operations—to take just a few obvious examples—the trial judge would immediately be enmeshed in disputes that could ripen into deeply troubling constitutional confrontations. Moreover, even seemingly minor changes in the President's schedule are imbued with significant portent by observers, both foreign and domestic. It is, therefore, not uncommon for a President to seek to maintain a pretense of "business as usual" to mask an impending crisis, while simultaneously having to attend to the urgent matter at hand. [In a footnote to this point, Bennett writes: "The experiences of Presidents Carter and Reagan provide dramatic examples: When the invasion of Grenada was being planned, President Reagan was week-ending at a Georgia golf club. He wanted to hurry back to Washington, but his advisors told him 'that a change in [his] schedule might draw

attention to the possibility of U.S. intervention.' He decided to remain in Georgia, but participated in meetings by way of telephone." The account is from the book *President Reagan—The Role of a Lifetime*, by Lou Cannon. Bennett added, "Similarly, during the 1980 mission to rescue the hostages in Iran, President Carter wanted to spend every moment monitoring the progress of the rescue mission, but had to stick to his regular schedule and act as though nothing of the kind was going on." This is from the book *Keeping Faith: Memoirs of a President*, by Jimmy Carter.] In such circumstances, simply having to ask a court for a change in the litigation schedule obviously could be highly damaging.

Even in areas not involving sensitive foreign or domestic concerns, a trial court would, under the [court of appeals'] "case management" approach, be able to second-guess judgments that are properly made only by the President. A myriad of important Presidential activities might warrant a change in a litigation schedule: foreign or domestic travel; contacting members of Congress to persuade them to vote for legislation; meetings with groups of citizens to call public attention to an issue; intensive briefings from advisors on complex subjects. If the President moved for a change in the litigation schedule to accommodate these interests, the denial of such a motion would effectively preempt the priorities of the Executive Branch.

This was the heart of Bennett's argument to the Court. He put all of his legal eggs in the separation-of-powers basket. In fact, during oral argument before the Court on January 13, 1997, four and a half months before the Court's decision, he told the justices right near the start of his argument: "I think this is a separation-of-powers case." Confirming that separation of powers was his only argument, Bennett told the media on May 27, 1997, the day the Court handed down its decision: "While we wish that the Supreme Court had accepted our separation-of-powers argument, we are confident the case ultimately will be resolved in the president's favor."

But the separation-of-powers argument by Bennett about one branch of government intruding upon another, though a valid argument, was as weak (weak, that is, relative to the main argument—balancing of interests—that should have been made) as it was elegant, and the Court disposed of it quickly and easily. After saying it was the strongest argument that Bennett had *made* (not that was *available*, however, as we shall see) to support the president's claim of temporary immunity, the Court showed just how strong they thought the argument was, treating it as a non sequitur, about as much of an intellectual put-down as there can be. Reiterating that they accepted the initial premise of Bennett's argument, they said: "It does not follow [i.e., it's a non sequitur], however, that separation of powers principles would be violated by allowing this action to proceed. The doctrine of separation of powers is concerned with the allocation of official power among the three co-equal Branches of our Government. The framers built into the tripartite Federal Government . . . a self-executing safeguard against the encroachment or aggrandizement of one branch at the expense of the other."

The Court went on to cite the case of *Buckley v. Valeo*, 424 U.S. 1 (1975), where the Court said: "[I]t is . . . clear from the provisions of the Constitution itself, and from the Federalist Papers, that the Constitution by no means contemplates total separation of each of these three essential branches of Government. The President is a participant in the lawmaking process by virtue of his authority to veto bills enacted by Congress. The Senate is a participant in the appointive process by virtue of its authority to refuse to confirm persons nominated to office by the President. The men who met in Philadelphia in the summer of 1787 were practical statesmen, experienced in politics, who viewed the principle of separation of powers as a vital check against tyranny. But they likewise saw that a hermetic sealing off of the three branches of Government from one another would preclude the establishment of a nation capable of governing itself effectively."

The Court in the Paula Jones case continued: "As [James] Madison [in the *Federalist Papers*, no. 47] explained, separation of powers does not mean that the branches 'ought to have no partial agency in, or no control over the acts of each other.' The fact that a federal court's exercise of its traditional Article III jurisdiction may significantly burden the time and attention of the Chief Executive is not sufficient to establish a violation of the Constitution . . . [I]t is settled law that the separation-of-powers doctrine does not bar every exercise of jurisdiction over the President of the United States. . . . If the Judiciary may severely burden the Executive Branch by reviewing the legality of the President's *official* conduct . . . it must follow that the federal courts have power to determine the legality of his *un*official conduct. . . . We therefore hold that the doctrine of separation of powers does not require federal courts to stay all private actions against the President until he leaves office."

Since the separation-of-powers argument was for all intents and purposes the only argument made on behalf of the president's position, it was time to turn off the lights for the president's cause.

Unbelievably, the president's lawyers went from the argument of the public interest in the effective functioning of the presidency, which the Court said had merit, to the separation-of-powers argument of pitting the president (executive branch of government) against the judicial branch of government, as opposed to doing what is invariably done in cases like this; namely, pitting the *public* interest against the *private* interest (here, Paula Jones's desire to have her case proceed to trial without further delay). They were like someone, say, at a fair, who gets inside the gate, but then, instead of proceeding forward to the main attractions, inexplicably takes a sharp left or right turn—a detour or tributary, as it were, that takes them off to the weed-choked fringes of the fairgrounds where the trailers and the support equipment for the main attractions are located. That is, instead of going on to make the very strongest argument available to them, the president's lawyers made the weakest.

As an aside, Bennett may have been seduced into making separation of powers the basis for his temporary-immunity argument simply because the district court in Little Rock, the court of appeals in St. Louis, and others had proclaimed, without offering strong support, that it is the constitutional font from which immunity, if it exists, springs. "Whatever immunity the President enjoys flows by implication from the separation of powers doctrine, which itself is not mentioned in the Constitution, but is reflected in the division of powers among the three branches. See U.S. Constitution, Articles I, II, III," the court of appeals said. In fact, in granting the president temporary immunity, the district court had earlier said it had "sought to give effect to the full meaning of the separation of powers doctrine originally enunciated by Montesquieu and implicit in the founding fathers' structure of the Constitution."[11]

But like other courts that have made this argument, neither the appellate court nor the district court went on to explain why the source of immunity is the doctrine of separation of powers. What reasoning dictates that if a president is immune from civil liability, the immunity has to come from the fact that there are three branches of government? Maybe the reason the courts don't give any rationale for their gratuitous observation is that there is none. From a relative standpoint, there are very few Supreme Court cases where presidential immunity and separation of powers are even discussed, and those that there are, like the 1982 case of *Nixon v. Fitzgerald*, 457 U.S. 731 (which granted absolute immunity to presidents for lawsuits arising out of their official duties), invariably cite *U.S. v. Nixon*, 418 U.S. 683 (1974) as authority. In *U.S. v. Nixon*, the Watergate special prosecutor sought certain tapes and documents relating to conversations and meetings between the president and his aides which were needed as evidence in the criminal trial of these former aides. They were charged with attempting to obstruct justice by covering up White House involvement in the 1972 break-in at the Democratic National Committee headquarters. President Nixon filed a motion to quash the subpoena for these tapes and documents on the ground of "executive privilege." The Supreme Court said that a "President and those who assist him must be free to explore alternatives in the process of shaping policies and making decisions and to do so in a way many would be unwilling to express except privately. These are the considerations justifying a presumptive privilege for Presidential communications. The privilege is fundamental to the operation of Government and inextricably rooted in the separation of powers under the Constitution." However, the Court held that this "presumptive privilege" was overcome by the compelling need in a *criminal* case, as the *Nixon* case was, "to develop all relevant facts . . . To ensure that justice is done, it is imperative . . . that compulsory process be available for the production of evidence needed either by the prosecution or by the defense."

So in *Nixon*, the case cited for the proposition of presidential immunity derived from the separation of powers, the Court was dealing only with the narrow issue of whether the president's papers and communications, once a lawsuit has already been filed and is going forward, are privileged and protected from compulsory production, not the much larger issue of whether in the first instance he can be civilly sued or criminally prosecuted for his alleged misconduct. Moreover, the *Nixon* Court held that the president did *not* have such protection under the circumstances of that case.

In any event, as we have seen, the Supreme Court in the Paula Jones case virtually dismissed the separation-of-powers argument out of hand.

After the Supreme Court rejected Bennett's separation-of-powers argument, it went on to give a sop to the president, stating: "Although we have rejected the argument that the potential burdens on the President violate separation of powers principles, those burdens are appropriate matters for the District Court to evaluate in its management of the case. The high respect that is owed to the Office of the Chief Executive, though not justifying a rule of categorical immunity, is a matter that should inform the conduct of the entire proceeding, including the timing and scope of discovery." Big deal. Courts do that for people the public has never heard of, and they are particularly sensitive to a defendant's schedule if he or she is a prominent person, such as a city official, an executive of a large corporation, or a top athlete. In fact, with respect to the latter, judges are apt to go far beyond just being sensitive and accommodating. Show me a judge in Chicago, for instance, who would not postpone the trial of a civil lawsuit against Michael Jordan until the end of the entire season, if for no other reason than to avoid a lynching by the people of Chicago. In other words, the Court gave the president of the United States *nothing at all.*

Lest anyone think that the Court's directing the trial judge to evaluate the burdens on the president in its management of the case, including the timing and scope of discovery, included the possibility of the trial judge continuing the case until after the president leaves office, the Court made it very clear it had no such thing in mind. "It was an abuse of discretion," the Court went on to say, "for the District Court [trial judge] to defer the trial until after the President leaves office," adding that the district court should "schedule the trial promptly after discovery is concluded." And as of the writing of this book, the trial judge has already set a trial date of May 27, 1998.[12]

The main issue that should have been raised by the president's lawyers in the Paula Jones case, and the one that the Court, on its own, should have dealt with, is whether or not the American public's interest in the effective functioning of the office of the presidency outweighed the private interest of Paula Jones in having her lawsuit go to trial without further delay. This is the time-honored and unavoidable balancing-of-interests test that the U.S. Supreme Court, as well as inferior courts, has been routinely using for over two centuries.

Many times in a lawsuit, only one side has a valid and legally protectible interest. But when a Court is confronted with two valid but conflicting interests (Jones's interest in having her case brought to trial now, and the public's interest in having the president devote *all* of his time and energies to effectively carry out the duties of his office they elected him to perform), what other way is there to resolve the matter other than by balancing the interests to see which interest is the one entitled to the most protection? By flipping a coin? Or perhaps by the Court's adopting the sandbox mentality of children and saying, "The last time an immunity case came before us, we ruled in favor of the public interest, so now it's the private interest's turn"?[13] Although I am not, as I've said, a constitutional scholar, I know of no other case than this one where the Court conceded a public interest yet failed to balance it against the interest of the individual who was the opposing party to the lawsuit. And when I asked a constitutional law professor, he too had never heard of another such case.[14]

It should be noted that I am not elevating the term *balancing of interests* to constitutionally imperative heights here—that if the Court in the Paula Jones case never used these magic words, their opinion is fatally defective as a matter of law. I'm obviously criticizing them for their failure to balance the interests, not for their failure to use the term. Nowhere in their decision did they indicate, by any *other* language, that they balanced the interests and concluded that Paula Jones's right to go to trial *now* was more important than the public's right to have the president they elected perform his duties without being diverted, not just physically (by his physical presence at meetings with his lawyers, depositions, and the trial) but mentally and emotionally by a very vexatious and highly embarrassing lawsuit. If any court actually balances the interests, they go on to say that one interest outweighs, or is more compelling, transcends, or is superior to the other (many examples will be given shortly). Not only didn't the Court in this case explicitly mention balancing the public interest against the private interest, or any equivalent language, they did not indicate in any way whatsoever that they gave any thought at all to this well-established legal doctrine. Since they used no language at all to indicate that they grappled in their minds with the core issue in this case, the most reasonable assumption is that they *didn't* grapple with it. It appears that on the need to balance interests to resolve the issue of temporary immunity, their minds, for whatever reason, were on sabbatical. If we're to take what the Court said and did at face value, they seemed to look at the public interest in an isolated fashion and, without bothering to compare it to the private interest of Paula Jones to determine which was the more important, simply concluded they could find no legal justification for postponing the trial. When looking at Paula Jones's interest, they again looked at it by itself and concluded that, like any other private American citizen who is suing for monetary damages, *in effect* (they didn't expressly say it) she had an *absolute* right to have her case tried without delay. "Like every other citizen . . . respondent [Paula Jones] has a right to an orderly disposition of her claims" is the way the Court put it in the last paragraph of its decision. But we will soon see, with several examples, that *no* right in our society, not even freedom of speech, is absolute.

Here's the proof that you *have* to balance interests. Say this suit occurred during wartime, the nation was in a death struggle with a formidable foreign power, and the president, as commander in chief of the armed forces, devoted almost all of his waking hours, as did Churchill and FDR in the Second World War, to the conduct of the war. Should Paula Jones, in the middle of all this, and with the lives and freedom of every citizen of this nation at stake, be permitted to take the president to trial for a month, or even a week, on these sexual harassment charges? The universal response could be capsulized with these words: "Well, come on. In *that* type of situation, obviously no."

Likewise, say this was a case, as so many are, that might tie the president up at the trial for six months, or even an entire year (e.g., a very complicated financial case with a great number of documents and witnesses). Again, the response would be, "Well, come on. In *that* type of situation, obviously no." But you see, the moment you say, "Well, come on," you are necessarily conceding that there are exceptions to Jones's right. And when you admit this, you are concomitantly admitting that her right is *not* an absolute one, as the Court—by its ruling and the language it used in support of the ruling—in effect held her right to be. And if a right is not absolute, this means that whether it can be exercised in a given situation necessarily requires a consideration of other interests. Once you are forced, by logic, to concede this, when you balance Jones's right to go to trial during the president's term in office against the public's right, even during peacetime, to have the president free of such an enormous distraction, the decision becomes a joke. Of *course* the public interest outweighs the private interest. It almost always does, even in cases, as we shall see, that are *much* less pronounced than this one. To hold otherwise would be to hold that the rights of an individual in a free and democratic society are more important than the conflicting rights of millions of individuals, an obvious absurdity. Inherent in the notion of democracy is that the majority rules. However, individual rights (privacy, property ownership, speech, religion, etc.) are protected by our government from the excesses of majority rule, no matter how unorthodox or distasteful their exercise may be to the majority, *but only as long as they don't impinge on the rights of others*. When they do, the rights have to be curtailed, that is, your right to swing your fist ends at the beginning of my nose. For instance, with respect to the First Amendment rights of freedom of speech and of the press, as Justice Brennan said in the companion cases of *Roth v. United States* and *Alberts v. California*, 354 U.S. 476 (1957): "All ideas having even the slightest redeeming social importance—unorthodox ideas, controversial ideas, even ideas hateful to the prevailing climate of opinion—have the full protection of [First Amendment] guarantees, *unless* excludable because they encroach upon . . . more important interests."

What conceivable argument could possibly be made for the proposition that Jones's right to proceed to trial now with her private lawsuit is more important than the public's right to have its president be undiverted and undistracted in the performance of his duties running the country? No one answered that question in the Jones case for the simple reason that *it was never even asked.* If it had been asked, what argument could have been made by those who wanted Jones's lawsuit to proceed? The platitude that no one is above the law? The problem is that that argument doesn't address itself to the balancing question. It is only another way of saying that Jones has the right to sue President Clinton and have her day in court, which no one, including the president, is contesting.

Does the shocking failure of President Clinton's lawyers in the Jones case to make the only strong argument the president had to secure a postponement (the argument that the Court, once *forced* to address it, would have found virtually impossible to reject) relieve the Supreme Court of all responsibility for their decision in this case? Obviously not. The Court has said many times (the first time in *Marbury v. Madison,* decided in 1803) that it has a duty to determine what the correct law in a case is. The fact that a litigant before it fails to raise relevant legal issues doesn't relieve the Court, in reaching its decision, of the obligation to consider those issues on its own, something it has done on countless occasions. The Court would never take the position that "gee, because the petitioner's (or respondent's) lawyers failed to make a legal argument that should have been made in this case, we're unfortunately forced to have to make a ruling that we know is bad law." In fact, the Court is so cognizant of, and opposed to, the incompetence of lawyers that it has, for instance, reversed criminal convictions of defendants because the incompetence of their lawyers prevented them from receiving a fair trial.

It is very important to note that the relief sought by the president in this case is not extraordinary; that is, it is not unprecedented for defendants in civil cases to have the lawsuit against them suspended, without the plaintiff's consent, for long periods. In the following situations (there are others), the defendant receives the benefit of a temporary immunity even though, like President Clinton in this case, no *official* act of the defendant is involved. For example, under 11 U.S.C.S. §362 (1978), with a few exceptions (e.g., a criminal action, action to establish paternity), the filing of a bankruptcy petition "operates as a stay . . . of [any] judicial, administrative or other action or proceeding against the debtor that was . . . commenced before" the filing of the petition. The stay covers even "the enforcement, against the debtor . . . of a judgment obtained before" the filing, and continues until the bankruptcy proceedings are terminated, which in many instances is several years. A 1977 House Judiciary Committee report on Section 362 concedes that other than the few specified exceptions, the scope of Section 362 "is broad. All proceedings are stayed," including "civil actions."

And because of the public's interest in justice and the enforcement of the criminal law, it is the policy in every state that a criminal trial against a defendant takes precedence over a civil lawsuit against the same defendant arising out of the same set of circumstances, even if the defendant were to waive his constitutional right to a speedy trial under the Sixth Amendment.[15] In many cases, this results in a postponement of the civil trial for several years. One example among thousands is the O.J. Simpson murder case, where the civil trial for wrongful death against Simpson by the survivors of Nicole Brown and Ronald Goldman had to be postponed for almost two years because the criminal trial took precedence.

Most analogous to the case of *Jones v. Clinton*, because of the rationale given for the deferral of the lawsuit, is the Soldier's and Sailor's Civil Relief Act of 1940, 50 U.S.C. App. §501–525, which expressly tolls (stays, suspends) civil claims against military personnel during the course of their active duty. Why? Section 510 provides that "provision is made to suspend enforcement of civil liabilities . . . of persons in the military service of the United States in order to enable such persons to *devote their entire energy to the defense needs of the nation.*" The statute goes on to say that this means "the temporary suspension of legal proceedings." As the court said in *Slove v. Strohm*, 236 N.E. 2nd 326 (1968), "the purpose of the Soldier's and Sailor's Civil Relief Act is to permit members of the Armed Forces to *devote their full attention* to the defense of the country." And in *Blazejowski v. Stadnicki*, 58 N.E. 2nd 164 (1944), the court said "the purpose of the act was to *ensure to those in the armed services a state of mind relatively at peace so far as the cares and burdens of civil litigation is concerned.*"

So even during peacetime, a soldier going through basic training at Fort Benning, Georgia, whose principal challenge is to learn how to assemble and disassemble an M-16 rifle, is legally entitled to a postponement of any civil action against him so that he can devote all his energy and attention to his duties, but the president of the United States, who has the most important and demanding job on earth, is not. Is this sense or nonsense? What previously recognized form of logic would allow this?

Could the argument be made that the only reason the Court in the Jones case did not grant the president the relief he sought is simply that Congress had enacted no statute expressly providing him (unlike military personnel) with such relief? ("If Congress deems it appropriate to afford the President . . . protection," the Court in the *Jones* case said in its opinion, "it may respond with appropriate legislation.") The answer to the question is no. As the Supreme Court itself said in *Nixon v. Fitzgerald*, where it granted absolute immunity to presidents for lawsuits arising out of their official acts, "a specific *textual* [that is, statutory] basis has *not* been considered a prerequisite to the recognition of immunity." If it were, the Court, in the Paula Jones case, wouldn't have devoted just one line in their entire opinion to the lack of a congressional statute in this case, and on the very last page of their opinion at that. It would have been a one-page opinion, and right off the top they would have simply said, with no need for further discussion, that they could not give the temporary immunity the president was seeking because there was no statute that provided such relief. And that would have been that. End of discussion. Instead, the Court wrote twenty-eight pages on the issue of whether they *should* give him the temporary immunity he sought, and decided against it. Nor does there need to be any *constitutional* basis for immunity. In *Butz v. Economou*, 438 U.S. 478 (1978), Economou brought an action against the secretary of agriculture and others under 42 U.S.C. §1983 (the same section Paula Jones sued President Clinton under) for attempting to revoke or suspend the registration of his commodity futures company. The Supreme Court held that the secretary and his assistants were entitled to absolute immunity, noting that "the doctrine of official immunity from §1983 liability . . . [is] not constitutionally grounded." If you don't need a constitutional basis for *absolute* immunity, you certainly don't need it for the smaller *temporary* immunity the president was seeking.

This was simply a case where the Court decided they did not want to grant the president temporary immunity. Their decision clearly was not based on the absence of a statute or constitutional provision providing said immunity. I mean, we know from the Court's history that they routinely create rights in our society where no statute or constitutional provision provides such rights. We need go no further than the law of immunity alone. In addition to the aforementioned cases of *Butz v. Economou* and *Nixon v. Fitzgerald*, the Court created absolute immunity for all judges—see *Pierson v. Ray*, 386 U.S. 547 (1967); state legislators—see *Tenney v. Brandhove*, 341 U.S. 367 (1951) (the absolute immunity of members of Congress, as opposed to state legislators, was not created by the Supreme Court; it is expressly provided for under the "speech or debate" clause of Article 1, Section 6 [1] of the U.S. Constitution); and even prosecutors—see *Imbler v. Pachtman*, 424 U.S. 409 (1976), for lawsuits arising out of their official duties, *even though neither a statute nor the Constitution provided such immunity.*[16]

In other words, *any* civil lawsuit filed against judges, legislators, and prosecutors for conduct arising out of their official duties will be automatically dismissed by the Court on the motion of the defendant, even where, as the Court said in *Pierson* (with respect to judges), "the judge is accused of acting maliciously and corruptly." The defendant judge, legislator, and prosecutor, then, has complete exemption from liability, and the rights of the individual plaintiff are permanently extinguished. (Again, in the Paula Jones case the president was seeking only a postponement, not an extinguishing, of her right to have her day in court.) For instance, in *Imbler*, the petitioner (Imbler) had been prosecuted and convicted of first-degree murder for the 1961 killing of the owner of a Pomona, California, market during a robbery and was sentenced to death. Thereafter, Imbler sought a writ of habeas corpus in a federal district court challenging the validity of his conviction. A hearing was held during which the main witness against Imbler recanted his identification of Imbler at the trial. At the hearing, the district court found eight instances of prosecutorial misconduct, six of which involved the testimony of this main prosecution witness against Imbler. The court said: "As to each of the six items of false testimony . . . the court finds that the prosecutor had knowledge of such falsity, or, if he did not have actual knowledge, that he had reason to believe such testimony was false, and his reckless use thereof in disregard of such reason is to be treated the same as the knowing use of false testimony."

After Imbler obtained his release on the writ of habeas corpus (based in part on newly discovered evidence by the prosecutor himself which was favorable to Imbler, and which the prosecutor brought to the attention of the governor of California), the district attorney elected not to retry Imbler. Imbler then filed a civil rights action in federal district court against the prosecutor under 42 U.S.C. §1983 (the same section Paula Jones sued under), alleging that the prosecutor, during the trial, had knowingly used false testimony and suppressed material evidence. The district court held that the prosecutor was immune from liability, and the court of appeals affirmed. The Supreme Court granted certiorari, and in affirming the holding of the two lower courts said: "To be sure, this immunity does leave the genuinely wronged defendant without civil redress against a prosecutor whose malicious or dishonest action deprives him of liberty. But the alternative . . . would disserve the broader public interest. It would prevent the vigorous and fearless performance of the prosecutor's duty that is essential to the proper functioning of the criminal justice system." As the Supreme Court realistically noted in *Nixon v. Fitzgerald,* "It never has been denied that absolute immunity may impose a regrettable cost on individuals whose rights have been violated. But . . . it is not true that our jurisprudence . . . supplies a remedy in civil damages for every legal wrong." This state of mind and candid appraisal of the real world, as opposed to blithely traipsing through the tulips of theory, certainly should have impelled the Court to at least grant a continuance to the president in the Paula Jones case, particularly where here, as opposed to the absolute immunity cases, there would be no extinguishing of Jones's right to have her day in court. Acting U.S. Solicitor General Walter Dellinger, in his amicus curiae (friend of the court) brief in support of the president's position, said, "Staying [this] private suit until the conclusion of the President's term of office prevents the diversion of the President's time and attention while preserving the plaintiff's right ultimately to obtain redress if her claims are determined to be meritorious."

It should not be forgotten that neither the plaintiff nor the defendant in a *civil* case has a constitutional right to a "speedy trial." That right is reserved only for defendants in *criminal* cases. (The Sixth Amendment provides: "In all criminal prosecutions the accused shall enjoy the right to a speedy and public trial.")

Does it make any difference that, as opposed to the absolute-immunity cases, *un*official conduct of the president was involved in the Paula Jones case? Why should it? Unofficial conduct in no way eliminates the need to balance the public against the private interest. If, as we have seen, unofficial conduct of military personnel, even buck privates, doesn't eliminate the need, why should it with the president of the United States? Moreover, in addition to the Court's reasoning in the absolute-immunity cases that the absence of said immunity would inhibit judges, legislators, and prosecutors from vigorously performing their duties properly because of fear of retaliation by those affected by their decisions, another critically important consideration, which the Supreme Court said militated in favor of their granting absolute immunity in these cases, was the Court's concern about time and energy distraction in the event of a lawsuit, the precise concern that the president's lawyers expressed in the Paula Jones case. In *Imbler*, the Court spoke about any trial against a prosecutor causing a "deflection of the prosecutor's energies from his public duties." In *Tenney*, the Court said that immunity for legislators avoids the problem of their being "subjected to the cost and inconvenience and distractions of a trial" resulting from a lawsuit against them. In *Pierson*, the Court said immunity was needed to avoid, for judges, the "burden" of litigation against them. In all three of these cases, the U.S. Supreme Court balanced the public interest against a private interest and granted immunity "for the benefit of the public" *(Pierson)*, so as not to "disserve the broader public interest" *(Imbler)*, "for the public good" *(Tenney)*.

As stated earlier, the Supreme Court, in *Nixon v. Fitzgerald*, also granted absolute immunity to the president for lawsuits arising out of his official duties to avoid the distraction of his time and energy. But as the district court in Little Rock in the Paula Jones case perceptively observed in originally granting President Clinton a postponement of the trial to the end of his term, "The concerns expressed by . . . the Supreme Court [in *Nixon v. Fitzgerald*, which said "Diversion of the President's energies by concern with private lawsuits would raise unique risks to the effective functioning of government"] are not lessened by the fact that these alleged actions preceded his Presidency, nor by the fact that his alleged actions would not have been within his official governmental capacity anyway. The problem, still, is essentially the same—the necessity to avoid litigation . . . which could conceivably hamper the President in conducting the duties of his office. This situation, as stated by Justice Powell in . . . *Nixon v. Fitzgerald*, could have harmful effects in connection not only with the President but with the nation in general."

Just as no one can be in two places at the same time, no mind can think about or concentrate on two different and separate things at the same time. Therefore, assuming that President Clinton is not possessed of supernatural powers, for the countless seconds and great number of minutes and hours he is tied up on the Paula Jones case with depositions, meetings with his lawyers, writing notes to himself and, above all, the trial itself, or at any other time he is thinking about this terribly embarrassing lawsuit, by definition he is diverting his mind and attention from his presidential duties. When he is thinking about the Paula Jones case, it is of course impossible for him to be applying his mind to the affairs of state—affairs that affect not just all Americans, but, in many instances, the citizens of the world. Robert Bennett pointed out to the Court in his legal brief, "Anything that significantly affects [the President] will affect the functioning of the Executive Branch as well." Walter Dellinger, in his amicus curiae brief, stated the problem presented by a private lawsuit against a sitting president well. Though this excerpt from his brief is a long one, I believe it is worth the space.

> As a practical matter, the countless issues of domestic and foreign policy that demand the President's attention fully occupy, and indeed outstrip, the capacity of the President to respond. . . . In the words of one scholar, "being President is a little like being a juggler who is already juggling too many balls and, at the most frustrating moments, is forever having

more balls tossed at him." . . . Another scholar has observed that the President "is expected to do too many jobs at once; he cannot give proper attention to them all." . . . As a result, the Presidency's most precious commodity is time, and one of the most vexing problems for the President and his staff is how to divide that time among the disparate issues that call for his attention. Deadlines rule the President's personal agenda, and the President typically faces deadlines enough to drain his energy and crowd his time regardless of all else. . . . Throughout the country's history, Presidents have remarked upon the overwhelming burdens of the Presidency. Our first President, George Washington, wrote that "the duties of my office . . . at all times . . . require an unremitting attention." [After eight years in office, Washington said: "I had rather be in my grave than endure another four years as President."] . . . President Jefferson explained that his duties "enjoined his constant agency in the concerns of 6 million people," and that during his annual vacation, "the public business . . . goes on and on as unremittingly." . . . President John Quincy Adams said that he could "scarcely conceive a more harassing, wearying . . . condition of existence." . . . President Polk complained that "the public have no idea of the constant accumulation of business requiring the President's attention." . . . President Theodore Roosevelt noted that "every day, almost every hour, I have to decide very big as well as very little questions." . . . President Taft noted that "one trouble is no sooner over in this office than another arises." . . . President Wilson stated that "the amount of work that a President is supposed to do is preposterous," and concluded that "my work can be properly done only if I devote my whole thought and attention to it and think of nothing but the immediate task at hand." . . . In the modern era of United States leadership as a world power, the responsibilities noted by earlier Presidents have only increased. President Truman concluded that "the pressures and complexities of the Presidency have grown to a state where they are almost too much for one man to endure." . . . President Eisenhower observed that "the duties of the President are essentially endless. No daily schedule of appointments can give a full timetable—or even a faint indication—of the President's responsibilities. Entirely aside from the making of important decisions, the formulation of policy through the National Security Council and the Cabinet, cooperation with the Congress and with the States, there is for the President a continuous burden of study, contemplation and reflection." . . . President Lyndon Johnson recounted that "of all the 1,886 nights I was President, there were not many when I got to sleep before one or two A.M., and there were few mornings when I didn't wake up by six or six-thirty."

The ultraconservative wing of the Republican Party, if they had a patriotic bone in their body, which they do not, would want the president, even though he is a Democrat, to do well. Why? Because if he does well, so does the country. But since these beady-eyed, narrow-minded people, at bottom, really don't care how the country does—they only want the country to do well if one of their people is president—they wish, encourage, and promote all kinds of harm on the president, even on his wife, Hillary. Not only would they actually be very *happy* if the president, whose time is extremely precious, was tied up for months on the Paula Jones case, to the detriment of the country, they'd also love nothing better than to see him humiliated, even though this humiliation would automatically and necessarily be humiliating to this entire country in the eyes of the world. This is the crowd that can frequently be heard to say, "He's not *my* president." The same people whose generational predecessors, particularly in the South, celebrated when President Kennedy and Martin Luther King were assassinated. What does it say about a group of vile, mean-spirited, and indecent people like this when the best defense for their attitude and behavior, if there is one, is that they are cretinous?

I was speculating earlier that perhaps one of the reasons why the media is harsher on Democratic leaders than on Republicans (we have to exclude President Nixon, where the country learned, unequivocally, that the president was actively engaged in criminal conduct) was that they were trying to kiss up to the far right, trying to let them know they're really not as bad as the far right thinks they are. But I have news for them. There's no way to appease this flag-waving but thoroughly un-American, unpatriotic bunch. There's only one thing they can do to even *begin* to satisfy them, and that's to change their registration from Democrat to Republican. *That's more important to these people than anything else.* To these feeble-minded morons, being a Democrat is a cardinal sin, one that is an automatic ground for excommunication from their flag-waving religion. Do you think, for instance, this group would be insanely pursuing the Vince Foster matter—even after their own legal spear-carrier, Kenneth Starr, was forced to conclude in his report of October 10, 1997, that it was a suicide—if Clinton were a Republican? Indeed, if Clinton were a Republican, they wouldn't have pursued this matter, as well as a great many others, at all. The irony is that these right-wing Republican zanies have hurt the image of the Republican Party in the eyes of America's voters much more than the Democrats have, repelling moderates in both parties as well as thinking conservatives (no, the latter term is not necessarily a contradiction in terms).[17]

As indicated earlier, balancing (or weighing) of interests is a very old judicial doctrine used by all courts when there is a conflict between two competing interests. It is a doctrine born not out of any statute or even the Constitution, but out of common sense, and it imposes realism and practicality on popular clichés (e.g., "no one is above the law"), clichés that would otherwise be perpetuated and foisted upon us by such institutions as the *New York Times* and the *Washington Post*, which undeservedly enjoy the very highest intellectual reputation and esteem in our society.

Balancing of interests also, in many instances, lends realism and practicality to the unqualified language of the U.S. Constitution itself. For instance, the First Amendment provides categorically that "Congress shall make no law . . . abridging the freedom of speech." No wiggle room, right? But common sense tells us that no right is absolute, and if the language of the First Amendment were taken literally, there would be all manner of problems in our society. As Justice Holmes said in *Schenck v. United States*, 249 U.S. 47 (1918), "The most stringent protection of free speech would not protect a man in falsely shouting 'fire' in a theater, and causing a panic."

Likewise, the notion of equality among men is embodied in our Declaration of Independence ("We hold these truths to be self-evident, that all men are created equal"), and the Fourteenth Amendment to the Constitution unqualifiedly provides that "[n]o state shall . . . deny to any person within its jurisdiction the equal protection of the laws." But again, this language, out of common sense and necessity, cannot be taken literally. Laws discriminate against certain classes of people all the time and are held not to violate the Fourteenth Amendment as long as there's a reasonable basis for the discrimination. When we tax unequally, that is not treating everyone equally under the law, but the public need to pay the expenses of government, and the feeling that those who have more should shoulder the burden of taxation more than those less economically advantaged legally justifies the discrimination. After a comprehensive review of equal-protection cases under the Fourteenth Amendment, Joseph Tussman and Jacobus tenBrock wrote in 37 *California Law Review* 341 (1949): "It is clear [from the cases] that the demand for equal protection cannot be a demand that laws apply universally to all persons. The Legislature, if it is to act at all, must impose special burdens upon, or grant special benefits to, special groups or classes of individuals."

As the U.S. Supreme Court pointed out (*Barbier v. Connolly*, 113 U.S. 27 [1885]) in the classical statement of this view of the Fourteenth Amendment: "Neither the Fourteenth Amendment . . . nor any other Amendment was designed to interfere with the power of the State . . . to prescribe regulations to promote health, peace, morals, education, and good order of the people. . . . From the very necessities of society . . . special burdens are often necessary for general benefits . . . but they are designed, not to impose unequal or unnecessary restrictions upon anyone, but to promote, with as little inconvenience as possible, the general good." The "general good"— these are words, like "public interest" or "public welfare," that are a common thread running throughout all balancing-of-interests cases. It's a notion that the Supreme Court, in the Paula Jones case, clearly forgot all about. As Tussman and tenBrock articulate perceptively: "The Constitution does not require that things different in fact be treated in law as though they were the same. But it does require, in its concern for equality, that those who are similarly situated be similarly treated." Another indisputable notion that the Court, in the Paula Jones case, completely failed to consider.

In other words, although no one is above the law in our society under all circumstances, we *do* treat certain people differently because of circumstances or because of their station in life. For example, we usually treat juveniles and elderly people differently when they are charged with criminal offenses. People with children don't have to pay as much federal income tax as those without children. When you or I or the nine justices of the Supreme Court land at an airport, nothing is changed. But when the president of the United States does, the terminal at the airport where he lands is usually closed down, and when he goes from the airport to his destination in town, as opposed to you, me, and the justices, his motorcade proceeds through red lights.

The examples of the U.S. Supreme Court balancing or weighing the public interest against a private interest are virtually endless. The volumes containing decisions of the Supreme Court are lousy with such cases. (Likewise with lower courts around the land. As the Supreme Court said in *Piper Aircraft Company v. Reyno*, 454 U.S. 257 (1981), "[W]here the [trial] court has considered all relevant public and private interest factors, and where its balancing is reasonable, its decision deserves substantial deference.") The following few are merely illustrative. Note the frequent use by the Court of words such as "duty," "must," "necessarily," and "requires" in reference to the need and unavoidability of balancing the interests.

Perhaps no right in our society is more fundamental and cherished, and more responsible for our being a great nation, than freedom of speech, the crown jewel in the tiara of rights guaranteed to all Americans under the first ten amendments (Bill of Rights) to the U.S. Constitution. As opposed, for instance, to the horrors of Communism in Stalin's Soviet Union, an American citizen can get up on an orange crate in the town square and without any fear of retribution shout out that our president is a despicable, swinish lout who should be impeached and locked up.[18] Freedom of speech has been described as the most important of all our freedoms because "all other rights are dependent on it." Even the great wit and iconoclast H. L. Mencken, whose credo seemed to be "whatever it is, I'm against it," genuflected when it came to this First Amendment right.

"Almost the only thing I believe in with a childlike and unquestioning faith, in this world of doubts and delusions," he wrote, "is free speech." But the cases where even this great freedom has been abridged because of the public interest are legion.

In *United Steel Workers of America v. National Labor Relations Board*, 339 U.S. 382 (1949), officers of a union contended that the requirement of the Management Labor Relations Act that each union officer state in an affidavit that he did not believe in and was not a member of any organization that believes in or teaches the forceful overthrow of the U.S. government infringed upon their First Amendment right of free speech. The Supreme Court, after balancing the interests, sustained the constitutionality of the act, stating: "When particular conduct is regulated in the interest of public order and . . . results . . . in abridgment of speech, the duty of the courts is to determine which of these two conflicting interests demands the greater protection." In a similar holding, the Supreme Court said in *Barenblatt v. United States*, 360 U.S. 109 (1959): "Where First Amendment rights are asserted to bar governmental interrogation, resolution of the issue *always* involves a balancing by the courts of competing private and public interests."

In *Chaplinsky v. New Hampshire*, 315 U.S. 568 (1941), Chaplinsky shouted at the city marshal near the entrance of the city hall in Rochester, New Hampshire, "You are a God damned racketeer" and "a damned Fascist, and the whole Government of Rochester are Fascists or agents of Fascists." He was convicted of violating a state statute prohibiting offensive, derisive language in public and appealed his conviction on the grounds it violated his freedom of speech. The Supreme Court upheld his conviction: "Such utterances are no essential part of any exposition of ideas, and . . . any benefit that may be derived from them is clearly *outweighed* by the social interest in order and morality."

So the right to speak freely, even though it's the most important right in our society, is not absolute—but the right to sue the president of the United States and have the lawsuit tried right in the middle of his term apparently is.

In a July 4, 1997, letter to the editor of the *New York Times*, the writer, a lawyer, stated that "in a balancing contest, the state invariably wins. That is the genius of the Constitution." However, although a balancing of the public against the private interest nearly always results in the public interest prevailing, this is not always true. A classic example is the case of *Rankin v. McPherson*, 483 U.S. 378 (1987), a case I want to discuss in a fair amount of depth because it is revealing on several levels. McPherson was a nineteen-year-old black woman who on January 12, 1981, was appointed a deputy in the office of the constable of Harris County, Texas, and put on a ninety-day probationary period. On March 30, 1981, when she heard on an office radio of the attempted assassination of President Ronald Reagan, she and her boyfriend, a coworker, had a brief, private conversation in which she said she had thought it would have been a black person who would shoot the president. When her boyfriend said, "Yeah, he's cutting back on Medicaid and food stamps," she said, "Yeah, welfare and CETA. If they go for him again I hope they get him." Another deputy overheard this last remark and reported it to Constable Rankin, who fired McPherson. She brought suit against Rankin and the county, contending she was denied her First Amendment right of freedom of speech.

The Supreme Court agreed, holding that the issue "*requires* a balance between the interest of the employee, as a citizen . . . and the interest of the State, as an employer, in promoting the efficiency of the public services it performs through its employees." The Court noted that although McPherson's title was "deputy constable," this was the case only because all employees of the office, regardless of job function, were deputy constables. The Court said that McPherson "was not a commissioned peace officer, did not wear a uniform, and was not authorized to make arrests or permitted to carry a gun. [Her] duties were purely clerical [and] her work station was a desk at which there was no telephone, and in a room to which the public did not have ready access."

The Court said that under the circumstances there was no evidence that McPherson's remark "interfered with the efficient functioning of the office." (The Court added that although "a threat to kill the President would not be protected by the First Amendment . . . McPherson's statement did not amount to a threat.") The Court concluded that "in applying [the] balancing test . . . we are not persuaded that [the county's] interest in discharging [McPherson] *outweighed* her rights under the First Amendment."

This would appear to be a clear case of the private right of freedom of speech (in this case, saying something similar to what millions of Americans, throughout the years, unfortunately have said about other public officials[19]) outweighing the public interest. Who could possibly disagree with the balancing in this case? None other than Justice Antonin Scalia, the judicial champion of the far right. He wrote a vigorous dissent in *Rankin v. McPherson*, and lo and behold, we learn from his dissent that Justice Scalia indeed *does* know all about the balancing-of-interests doctrine, saying the issue in the case was "whether [Rankin's and the county's] interest in preventing the expression of such statements . . . outweighed [McPherson's] interest in making the statement." Scalia concluded it did, asserting that McPherson was a member of a law-enforcement office and therefore "it boggles the mind to think that she had such a right."

Now, there's a justice who knows what is and what is not important in America—obviously someone with a high IQ and perhaps more degrees than a thermometer, but apparently no common sense whatsoever. One thing I have seen over and over again in life is that there is virtually no correlation between intelligence and common sense. IQ doesn't seem to translate that way. Here is Scalia on his hind legs, stridently balancing the interests in favor of the right of the constable in a county in Texas to fire an employee even though the constable had testified, per the majority opinion in the case, "that the possibility of interference with the functions of the Constable's office had not been a consideration in his discharge of respondent and that he did not even inquire whether the remark had disrupted the work of the office." But when it comes to the right of the president of the United States to perform his constitutional duties effectively and unencumbered, the unreconstructed right-wing ideologue was as silent as a cigar-store Indian, joining with his colleagues in the Paula Jones decision.[20] In Scalia's universe, the public has more of an interest in ensuring that private citizens in private conversations are not able to muse to friends about wishing the president were dead than in ensuring that the leader of this nation be able to run the affairs of state without a private lawsuit substantially diverting his attention, time, and energies from his official duties. And this is apparently the type of mentality that is sitting on the highest court in the land.

Balancing of interests applies to *all* cases before the Court where there is a conflict between valid interests, regardless of the nature of the case. A few more illustrative examples: In *O'Connor v. Ortega*, 480 U.S. 709 (1987), officials at a state hospital became concerned about possible improprieties on the part of a staff doctor who managed the hospital's psychiatric residency program. After his being placed on paid administrative leave, hospital officials searched his office and seized several items. The doctor brought suit, alleging that the search violated his Fourth Amendment right against "unreasonable searches and seizures." The Supreme Court upheld the constitutionality of the search, stating that "in the case of searches conducted by a public employer, we *must* balance the invasion of the employee's legitimate expectations of privacy against the government's need for supervision, control, and the efficient operation of the workplace." The Court held that the government's interest outweighed the private interest here.

In *United States v. Martinez-Fuerte*, 428 U.S. 543 (1976), the defendant, traveling by vehicle from Mexico to the United States, was arrested at a permanent immigration checkpoint operated by the border patrol when he was found to be illegally transporting aliens in his vehicle into this country. He appealed his subsequent conviction on the grounds of a violation of the Fourth Amendment. Affirming the conviction, the Court said it had "*weighed* the public interest [in conducting searches at the border] against the Fourth Amendment interest of the individual" and concluded the public interest outweighed the private interest. The Court went on to say that "other traffic-checking practices involve a different balance of public and private interests."

In *National Treasury Employees Union v. Von Rabb*, 109 S. Ct. 1384 (1989), the union sought an injunction against the Customs Service's drug testing program, asserting it was a violation of their rights under the Fourth Amendment. The Supreme Court, ruling against the union, said that "the Government's need to conduct the suspicionless searches required by the Customs program *outweighs* the privacy interest of employees engaged directly in drug interdiction."

In *California v. American Stores Company*, 495 U.S. 271 (1990), the defendant, a supermarket chain, sought to merge with a competitor by acquiring all of the latter's outstanding stock. The state of

California sought to enjoin the merger by alleging that it violated federal antitrust statutes. The federal district court's injunction was set aside by the U.S. Court of Appeals. The Supreme Court reversed the court of appeals, holding that the injunction was proper. Balancing the "public interest and private needs" here, the Court said that the otherwise "normal right [of the supermarket chain] to integrate the operations of the two previously separate companies" had to be enjoined because it could result in economic harm to California consumers.

In *Agins v. City of Tiburon*, 447 U.S. 255 (1979), Agins had acquired five acres of unimproved land for residential development. Before he commenced construction, the city of Tiburon, California, adopted zoning ordinances that allowed Agins to build only between one and five single-family residences on the land. Agins brought suit, alleging that the municipal zoning ordinances were unlawfully taking his property without just compensation in violation of his rights under the Fifth and Fourteenth Amendments. The Supreme Court said that determining whether or not there was such a violation "necessarily *requires* a weighing of private and public interests." Ruling against Agins, the Court held that the city's interest in protecting "the residents of Tiburon from the ill effects of urbanization" outweighed the private interest of Agins.

If you balance the interests when an individual's interest conflicts with a city *(Agins v. City of Tiburon)* or state *(California v. American Stores Company)*, under what conceivable theory don't you balance the interests when, as in the Paula Jones case, the individual's interest conflicts with the national interest? Actually, as we've seen from several of the cases cited in this section, the Supreme Court *does* balance the interests when an individual's rights conflict with a national interest. They just failed to do it, curiously, in the Paula Jones case.

It should be noted that Justice Stevens, who at least by his written words gave no indication at all in the Paula Jones case that he was aware of the balancing-of-interests doctrine, wrote the opinion in *California v. American Stores Company*. In fact, just one month after the Jones decision, in the case of *Reno v. American Civil Liberties Union*, 117 S. Ct. 2329 (1997), Justice Stevens, writing for the majority, struck down as unconstitutional the Communications Decency Act of 1996, which made it a crime to knowingly send or display "indecent" material over the Internet because children could see it. Though in sympathy with the act's purpose, Stevens wrote, "[T]he [public] interest in encouraging freedom of expression in a democratic society *outweighs* any theoretical but unproven benefit of censorship [of the individual]."

And in *Snepp v. United States*, 444 U.S. 507 (1979), Stevens, in discussing a CIA employment agreement in which the employee had agreed not to publish information or material relating to the agency without prepublication clearance, wrote that such "agreements in restraint of an individual's freedom of trade . . . are enforceable only if they can survive scrutiny under the 'rule of reason.' That rule, originally laid down in the seminal case of *Mitchell v. Reynolds*, 1 P.Wms. 181, 24 Eng. Rep. 347 (1711), requires . . . that the employer's interest not be *outweighed* by the public interest."[21]

So even way back in 1711 in jolly old England, before this nation even had a Supreme Court (1790), long before this nation's Civil War (1861–1865), Constitution (1789), or Declaration of Independence (1776), even over half a century before the stirrings for the American Revolution began (1764), courts in England were employing common sense ("rule of reason") and balancing the public interest against private interests. But not in 1997, here in the United States, in the case of Paula Jones v. President Clinton.

The courts, then, have to balance interests in *all* cases where there is a conflict between two protectible rights, and immunity cases are no exception. In *Nixon v. Fitzgerald*, the 1982 Supreme Court case that gave absolute immunity to presidents for lawsuits arising out of their official acts, the Court said that "absolute immunity merely precludes a particular *private* remedy for alleged misconduct in order to advance compelling *public* ends." Chief Justice Burger, in his concurring opinion, wrote, "Constitutional adjudication often bears unpalatable fruit. But the needs of a system of government sometimes must *outweigh* the right of individuals to collect damages." In Bennett's written petition to the Court, he relied heavily for his separation-of-powers argument on *Nixon v. Fitzgerald*, which cited the earlier case of *United States v. Nixon* for the proposition that the presumptive privilege for presidential communications is "rooted in the separation of powers under the Constitution." But the very next words in *Fitzgerald* were these: "But our cases also have established that a Court *must balance* the constitutional weight of the interest to be served against the dangers of intrusion on the authority and functions of the Executive Branch." In other words, even where the argument is separation of powers, the Court *still* has to balance the interests. Likewise, in Chief Justice Burger's concurring opinion in *Fitzgerald*, he went from separation-of-powers language ("invasion of the Executive function by the Judiciary") immediately into the balancing of interests, saying that in previous decisions the Court had granted absolute immunity to legislators, prosecutors, and judges, because "the public interest . . . *outweighs* the need for private redress." The Court in *Fitzgerald* (who was suing President Nixon and others, claiming he lost his job as a management analyst for the Department of the Air Force as retaliation for his testimony before a congressional committee concerning cost overruns in the defense industry) ruled in favor of immunity for President Nixon "in the case of this purely private suit for damages based on a President's official acts."

So even if Bennett did not focus on balancing of interests as the principal reason for granting a postponement of the trial to the president, the Court itself should have realized that the very language of its own decision in *Fitzgerald* ("must balance"), as well as in a great number of other previous cases, *demanded* a balancing of interests.

Although already alluded to in this book, perhaps a more in-depth discussion is called for here as to what the "public interest" was in the Paula Jones case that should have been balanced against the private interest of Paula Jones. For all intents and purposes, once a person becomes president of the United States, he belongs, if you will, to the nation, and the American people have a vested interest in his performing his duties well. "The Presidency is inseparable from the individual who is President," Bennett pointed out in his brief. Quoting George E. Reedy, press secretary for President Lyndon Johnson, Bennett added that "the President, for all practical purposes . . . affords the only means through which we can act as a nation." One example, among a great many, showing that the president belongs to the nation: Every week, Tuesdays through Saturdays, about 5,000 people a day trek through the White House, the home of the president and his family. According to the National Park Service, 1,079,783 people visited the White House in 1997. I wonder how many tourists trudged through the homes of the Supreme Court justices last year?

We call the president and his family the First Family. Even their pets are called the First Dog or the First Cat. As Justice Jackson said in *Youngstown Sheet and Tube Co. v. Sawyer*, 343 U.S. 579 (1952), the Constitution concentrates the executive authority in the president, "a single head in whose choice the whole nation has a part, making him the focus of public hopes and expectations. In drama, magnitude and finality his decisions so far overshadow any others that almost alone, he fills the public eye and ear." "The President, in the exercise of the executive functions," the Supreme Court said in *Langford v. United States*, 101 U.S. 341 (1879), "bears a nearer resemblance" to a king than does "any other Branch of Government."

The president's duties, the most important of which are set forth in Article 2, Section 2, of the U.S. Constitution, can perhaps best be summarized by saying that he is the leader of the country. As the nation's chief executive, he "runs" the country. In fact, he heads the executive (*execute,* i.e., "to carry out," "accomplish"—colloquially, "run") branch of government. (He is also universally recognized as the "leader of the free world.")

The daily headlines tell it all: "President Asks Senate to Okay Nuclear Test Ban"; "Clinton Pressing Both Sides to Settle U.P.S. Strike"; "Clinton Issues Guidelines for Religious Expression"; "Clinton to Chart Course for Better Ties with China"; "Clinton Wins Round in Congress on B-2 Bombers"; "President Signs Historic Vetoes"; "Clinton Orders New Drug Tests for Child Safety"; "Clinton Pressures States to Get People off Welfare"; "Clinton Embarks on Perilous Quest to Expand NAFTA"; "Clinton to Fight for National Academic Test"; "Citing Fraud in Home Care, Clinton Halts New Permits"; "Clinton Seeks First Balanced Budget in 30 Years"; "Clinton Calls on Japan at Summit to Lead Asia Out of Crisis"; "President Says U.S. Won't Join Treaty to Ban Mines—Says Ban Would Put G.I.'s at Risk"; "President Will Back Tougher Proposal to Rein in Smoking"; "Iran–Iraq Battles Lead Clinton to Rush

Carrier to Gulf"; "President Urges New Laws to Insure Safety of Foreign-Grown Crops Sold in U.S."; "Clinton Urges Quick Ban on Human Cloning"; "Clinton Heading for South America to Promote U.S. Trade"; "Clinton Supports Bill to Overhaul I.R.S."; "President Takes New Approach to Fight Global Warming"; "Clinton to Extend G.I. Role in Bosnia"; "President Imposes Import Ban on Assault Guns"; "Clinton to Push for Health Care Bill of Rights"; "President Signs Nuclear Pact with China."

Whether you agree or disagree with the president's politics, behind all these headlines, of course, are an enormous amount of study, reflection, and meetings with aides in the decision-making process. And every one of these decisions concerns a matter of consequence to the nation. In a December 1962 television interview, President John F. Kennedy related what his predecessor, Dwight D. Eisenhower, had said to him on the day of Kennedy's inauguration the year before: "There are no easy matters that will ever come to you as president. If they are easy, they will be settled at a lower level." Although the decisions the president must make are momentous, only he can make them. "Every final important decision has to be made right here on the President's desk," President Truman said. A sign on Truman's desk said it perfectly: "The buck stops here." Presidential scholar Clinton Rossiter says that Truman's sign sums up the essence of the presidency. "It is the one office in all of the land whose occupant is forbidden to pass the buck."

The president "must simultaneously conduct the diplomacy of a superpower, put together separate coalitions to enact every piece of legislation required by a vast and complex society, manage the economy, command the armed forces . . . respond to every emergency" is the way Godfrey Hodgson put it in his *All Things to All Men: The False Promise of the Modern American Presidency* (1980). He is, then, the chief policymaker for domestic and foreign affairs.

Since the lives of all American citizens are directly involved, no constitutional duty of the president's is more important than being commander in chief of our nation's armed forces. Moreover, he conducts, and makes the final decisions on, our nation's foreign policy. (Among other things, under Article 2, Section 2 [2], only he has the power, with the advice and consent of the Senate, "to make Treaties" [a contract between two or more nations]). Although the president frequently acts through his appointees and representatives at the State Department, as Rep. John Marshall (who would later become Chief Justice of the Supreme Court) said in a speech on the floor of the House of Representatives in 1800, "The President is the sole organ of the nation in its external relations. Of consequence, the demand of a foreign nation can only be made on him." So the decisions the president makes affect our relationship with all other nations of the world. Where was President Clinton when his aide, Bruce Lindsey, brought him the bad news of the Supreme Court's decision in the Paula Jones case on May 27, 1997? In Paris, being briefed for a private meeting with Russian president Boris Yeltsin over Russia's finally agreeing to the admission of Poland, Hungary, and the Czech Republic, three former Soviet satellites, to NATO, a historic breakthrough.

Can the president not only conduct foreign policy but *initiate* a war with a foreign nation? Although Article 2, Section 2 [1] does provide that "the President shall be Commander-In-Chief of the Army and Navy of the United States," technically this only places the president at the head of this nation's armed forces. It clearly envisions, as a predicate to his conducting war as the head of the nation's armed forces, that war has been declared. And Article 1, Section 8 [11] ("The Congress shall have power . . . to declare war") exclusively and unambiguously gives that power to Congress, not the president. So while no one disputes the inherent power of the president to engage the nation in war without first securing congressional approval in order to *repel* an invasion, the Constitution does not authorize the president to *initiate* war. As the United States Supreme Court as far back as *The Prize Cases*, 67 U.S. (2 Black) 635 (1863), said: "This is a Government created, defined, and limited by a written Constitution, every article, clause and expression in which was pondered and criticized, as probably no document in the affairs of men was ever before tested, refined and ascertained. . . . In this . . . Constitution, it was explicitly and exclusively declared, in words as plain as language affords, where this tremendous power should reside. To Congress is entrusted the power to declare war. . . . War is reserved to the judgment of Congress itself." The Court went on to say that the war power means that only Congress can "initiate war, put the country in the state of war."

Although the subject articles of the Constitution need no interpretation to determine the framers' intent, Alexander Hamilton, writing in 1788, a year before the Constitution went into effect, said: "[The] President is to be Commander-In-Chief of the Army and Navy of the United States. In this respect his authority would be nominally the same with that of the King of Great Britain, but in substance much inferior to it. It would amount to nothing more than a supreme command and direction of the land and naval forces, while that of the British King extends to the *declaring* of war . . . which by the Constitution would appertain to the Legislature."

So much for the interpretation of words and phrases, and the apparent intent of the framers of the Constitution. The reality is that throughout this nation's history presidents have time and again committed American military forces abroad *without* the approval of Congress. Although all presidents during their inauguration ceremonies swear to uphold the Constitution, when it comes to arguably the most serious and important (in terms of consequences) part of the Constitution—who has the right to commit the military forces of this nation to an armed conflict with another nation—most presidents, even self-proclaimed "strict constructionists" of the Constitution such as Ronald Reagan (Grenada, 1983) and George Bush (Panama, 1989), have cavalierly ignored the explicit constitutional language and their presidential oath. As political commentator Russell Baker has facetiously observed: "Presidents now say, sure, the Constitution gives Congress the right to declare war, but it doesn't forbid Presidents to *make* war, so long as they don't *declare* it. As a result, the declared war has become obsolete. Its successor is the undeclared war."

In a 1952 U.S. Supreme Court case dealing with a different use of presidential power, the dissent noted that even as of that date, forty-six years ago, there had been "125 incidents in our history in which Presidents, without Congressional authorization, and in the absence of a declaration of war, have ordered the armed forces to take action or maintain positions abroad." In fact, only five times in the nation's history has Congress declared war: the War of 1812; the Mexican War, 1846; the Spanish-American War, 1898; World War I, 1917; and World War II, 1941. In the recent Persian Gulf War, although Congress adopted resolutions authorizing the use of force (not quite the same as a declaration of war), the Bush administration flatly asserted it had the right to commit the nation to war without a congressional declaration of any kind. And a 1966 Department of State memorandum states: "Over a very long period in our history, practice and precedent have confirmed the constitutional authority [of the president] to engage United States Forces in hostilities without a declaration of war."

So presidents throughout our history (and even since the 1973 War Powers Resolution, 50 U.S.C. §1541–1548, a congressional act directing that presidents at least "consult with Congress") have for the most part not even bothered to seek congressional approval for the employment of military forces abroad.

Domestically, no congressional bill becomes a law unless the president signs it, or unless his veto is overridden by a two-thirds majority of Congress. Inasmuch as overriding presidential vetoes is difficult and rare—from a historical perspective, only about 3 percent of presidential vetoes have been overridden by Congress—essentially the president alone determines what all the new laws governing this nation will be. And since Article 2, Section 3, provides that the president "shall take care that the laws be faithfully executed," it is his ultimate responsibility to see that all federal laws, new and existing, are enforced.

The first task of a president upon being elected, of course, is to create his administration; that is, the body of officials through whom he will act. This enormous job continues, in the replacement and hiring of officials, on a daily basis throughout his presidency. And the president, after all, is a politician. That's how he became president. So during his first term he has to also concern himself with the practical reality of getting reelected. After all, he (along with his vice president) is the only public official for whom the entire nation votes, members of the House of Representatives and the Senate representing only state and local constituencies. As a politician, the president is also the leader of his political party, with all the considerable responsibilities that this suggests.

Perhaps no one ever described the demands on the president's time and the importance of the office of the presidency better and more succinctly than Akhil Amar and Neal Katyal in their article, "Executive Privileges and Immunities: The Nixon and Clinton

Cases," 108 *Harvard Law Review* 701 (1995): "Constitutionally speaking, the President never sleeps. The President must be ready, at a moment's notice, to do whatever it takes to preserve, protect, and defend the Constitution and the American people." In other words, the president, every waking hour, has to work on and deal with the problems Americans care most about in their daily lives, and you simply can't tie up and paralyze the presidency with private lawsuits. Just as the U.S. Supreme Court acknowledged in *Imbler v. Pachtman* (discussed earlier) that absolute immunity for judges, prosecutors, and legislators in the performance of their official duties is based on "considerations of public policy," these same public policy considerations should prohibit private lawsuits against presidents from being heard during the president's term. "Public policy" is a term that is not always easy to define and is ephemeral in that it varies with the changing habits, opinions, and welfare of the people. Moreover, what may be the public policy of one state may not be that of another. But generally speaking, public policy is the principle of law which holds that one should not be permitted to do anything that has a tendency to be injurious to the public or against the public good.

To make it more intellectually palatable to the insufferably theoretical purists (the type who once prompted President Lincoln to ask, "Is it possible to lose the nation and yet preserve the Constitution?") who reside in the rarefied, oxygenless atmosphere of the ivory tower, perhaps it would be availing to look at the problem from a different perspective. Bill Clinton is entitled to a temporary delay of the lawsuit not because of *who he is* but because of *what he does*, which is running the country as the people's elected president.[22] In other words, they should stop thinking about the president and start thinking about the presidency. I like the remark of former FBI and CIA director William Webster on *Nightline* (December 28, 1994) the evening of the ruling by the trial court in Little Rock continuing the case (but not pretrial discovery) until after the president's term. He said: "*We the people,* I think, won this victory, because we are entitled to a full-time president." The reason I like the remark is that implicit in it is the notion that the people of this nation, for all practical purposes, are a party to the lawsuit. Since their interests can be harmed by it, they are de facto defendants.

What makes the office of the presidency unique and far more

burdensome than any other office in our government is the fact that although the two other branches of our government are vested in a great number of people (Congress has 535 members; the Supreme Court and lower federal courts have 845 judges), our nation's founders consciously decided to vest the executive authority in one person rather than several. "The Executive Power shall be vested in *a* President of the United States of America," says Article II, Section 1 [1]. As Justice Breyer conceded in his concurring opinion in the Jones case, "[T]he President is not like Congress, for Congress can function as if it were whole, even when up to half of its members are absent, see U.S. Const., Art. I, Section 5, cl 1 ["a Majority of each [House] shall constitute a Quorum to do Business"]. It means that the President is not like the Judiciary, for judges often can designate other judges, e.g., from other judicial circuits, to sit [in their seat] . . . It means that, unlike Congress, which is regularly out of session . . . the President never adjourns. [Breyer could have added that not just Congress but all federal judges are normally "out of session" during weekday lunches, every evening and weekend, and all holidays and vacations, and the Supreme Court itself is normally in recess all of July, August, and September of each year, whereas the president is on duty every single hour of every day of the year] . . . Interference with a President's ability to carry out his public responsibilities is constitutionally equivalent to interference with the ability of the entirety of Congress, or the Judicial Branch, to carry out their public obligations." In a private letter President Thomas Jefferson wrote to United States Attorney George Hay on June 17, 1807, during a dispute over whether a federal court could compel him to appear as a witness in a criminal case (Jefferson refused), he noted that the executive branch "is the sole branch which the Constitution requires to be always in function." As former U.S. solicitor general Robert Bork has said: "The President is the only [constitutional] officer whose temporary disability while in office incapacitates an entire branch of government."

Aware of the singular importance of the presidency and the need to thereby protect its occupant, Alexander Hamilton felt the president should be temporarily immune not just from *civil* process (the issue in the Paula Jones case) but from the far more serious *criminal* process. *The Federalist* (commonly referred to as *The Federalist Papers*) is a collection of eighty-five essays written by Hamilton, James Madison, and John Jay under the *nom de plume* "Publius" between 1787 and 1788 in support of the proposed Constitution (which had been drafted in 1787 at the Constitutional Convention in Philadelphia) so it would be ratified by the requisite minimum nine out of the thirteen colonial states. The Constitution was of course ratified and went into effect in 1789. Though John Jay, a prominent New York City lawyer, did not participate in the Philadelphia Convention, Hamilton and Madison were among the most important framers of the Constitution, and therefore their essays are looked to by scholars to determine the "original intent" of the framers.

In *The Federalist* no. 69 (essay 69), Hamilton writes at page 446: "The President of the United States would be liable to be impeached, tried and, upon conviction of treason, bribery, or other high crimes or misdemeanors, removed from office; and would *thereafter* be liable to prosecution and punishment in the ordinary course of law."

In other words, even if the evidence were clear that a president had committed the crime of murder, it was the belief of Hamilton that he could not be arrested and prosecuted until *after* he was first impeached and removed from office following conviction by the Senate—that is, up until his removal he should have temporary immunity, as no other American citizen does, from ordinary criminal process. In a brief filed on behalf of the U.S. government by Solicitor General Robert Bork on October 5, 1973, in a Maryland federal district court regarding Vice President Spiro Agnew's claim of constitutional immunity from criminal process (which Bork said the vice president did not have), Bork embraced Hamilton's view, writing: "[The framers] assumed that the nation's Chief Executive, responsible as no other single officer is for the affairs of the United States, would not be taken from duties that only he can perform unless and until it is determined that he is to be shorn of those duties [through the impeachment process] by the Senate."

Lawrence Walsh, the Iran-Contra special prosecutor, seems to have taken it a step further, implying that certain crimes of the president should perhaps even be tolerated, overlooked. As is well known, although Walsh was vigorous in his investigation of Reagan and Bush administration officials for their involvement in the scandal, he was extraordinarily timid in his pursuit of Presidents Reagan and Bush themselves, never once seeking or even suggesting an indictment against either. This was so despite the fact that, among other evidence, the previously referred to notes of Secretary of Defense Caspar Weinberger (a man of recognized character and integrity who, along with Secretary of State George Shultz, was the only member of the Reagan administration who opposed Iran-Contra, but got caught up in attempting to protect the president) clearly showed that Reagan had violated federal laws in selling arms to Iran, a terrorist nation, in exchange for the release of American hostages, and Bush had lied in saying he was "out of the loop" on Iran-Contra. Walsh explained his timidity in a December 24, 1992, *MacNeil-Lehrer News Hour* interview. After saying that "President Reagan had deliberately violated the laws that prohibited his selling arms to Iran" and referring to then-President Bush's "own misconduct," when MacNeil asked him if he intended to prosecute Bush, Walsh answered, "I cannot comment on that." But he added deferentially: "The president of the United States is entitled to an area of tolerance. . . . The problems that he has are greater in scale, immensely greater, than any other government official. . . . A prosecutor should be very slow before he picks at a president, but that does not protect the secretary of defense or anyone else who carries out a policy by illegal means or tries to cover up a policy by illegal means."

To treat the president of the United States, as the Supreme Court did in the Paula Jones case, as no different from any other American when he is sued civilly for his unofficial conduct is idiotic on its face. He happens to be the most powerful, influential, and hence important person on the face of the earth. (Other than that little, incidental nugget of reality, I guess he's no different at all from you or me and therefore should be treated by the Supreme Court in the same exact way they would treat you or me. Right.) "There would appear no quality of the Presidency so impossible to deny as its massive power, over all the world of nations," Emmett John Hughes writes in his book *The Living Presidency* (1972). In a May 8, 1954, dinner speech,

President Truman said: "There's never been an office . . . in all the history of the world with the responsibility and the power of the presidency of the United States. That is the reason in this day and age that it must be respected . . . because it can mean the welfare of the world or its destruction."

Because he is the leader of this nation, whose actions routinely affect millions of Americans and sometimes billions of people the world over, common sense tells us that we have a public interest in protecting him to the extent that all of his time, attention, and energies can be directed toward the performance of his duties as chief executive. As Bennett (who cogently argued the public interest in the office of the presidency but failed to then go on and argue the legal necessity of balancing or weighing that interest against Paula Jones's private interest) said in his brief, "Anything that significantly affects [the president] will affect the functioning of the Executive Branch as well," and lawsuits, or even the threat of them, "distract a President from his public duties, to the detriment of not only the President . . . but also the nation that the Presidency was designed to serve." Indeed, as set forth earlier, a previous Supreme Court said in *Nixon v. Fitzgerald*, "Because of the singular importance of the President's duties, diversion of his energies by concern with private lawsuits would raise unique risks to the effective functioning of [our] Government."

But *this* Supreme Court did not agree. Syndicated columnist Suzanne Garment said that by the Court's decision and briskly dismissive treatment of the presidency, it was sending a clear message: "Being President does not make [one] very special or precious to the Republic, at least not special or precious enough to be excused from the ordinary aggravations of the legal process. . . . The importance of this unanimous judgment [is that] it points to a change in the standing of the Presidency among U.S. political institutions."

In the Court's determination not to give the president a temporary delay of the lawsuit, it even engaged in transparently strained reasoning. Inasmuch as the president has specifically enumerated powers granted to him under Article 2 of the U.S. Constitution, it necessarily follows that implicit within the grant is the unhampered ability to exercise these powers. As the Court said as early as *McCulloch v. Maryland*, 17 U.S. 316 (1819), "[T]hat which [is] reasonably appropriate and relevant to the exercise of a granted power [is] to be considered accompanying the grant." In *United States v. Nixon* the Court said that "the protection of the confidentiality of presidential communications" was among the powers and privileges that *flow from* the nature of enumerated powers. The Supreme Court time and time again has acknowledged the "implied" or "incidental" powers that inhere in the Constitution.[23] Supreme Court justice Joseph Story, who served on the Court for almost thirty-four years (1811–1845) and is perhaps the most respected and distinguished commentator on the Constitution, wrote in his oft-cited and influential *Commentaries on the Constitution of the United States* (1833) that these "incidental powers" of the president "must necessarily" include "the power to perform them without any obstruction or impediment whatsoever. The President cannot, therefore, be liable to arrest, imprisonment, or detention, while he is in the discharge of the duties of his office, and for this purpose his person must be deemed, in civil cases at least, to possess an official inviolability."

In the Paula Jones case, the Court performed an obvious tap dance to get around Story's assertion of a seemingly all-inclusive immunity in civil cases, drawing an unreasonable inference as to what his intent was. Justice Stevens wrote in a footnote: "Story said only that '*an* official inviolability' was necessary to preserve the President's ability to perform the functions of the office; he did not specify the dimensions of the necessary immunity." Therefore, the Court went on to conclude, denying the president temporary immunity for his unofficial acts, as opposed to his official ones, was not inconsistent with Story. But this is arbitrary and sophistic reasoning. Why should Story have to spell out the contours and dimensions of the immunity? His language clearly indicates *absolute* immunity. Whenever any absolute right (or prohibition) is given to someone, such as the license to drive a car, can it be later abridged ("Your license, son, doesn't specifically say you can drive this hopped-up car of yours on Highway 18 through my town, does it? That'll be a hundred-dollar fine, or I have a nice bed for you tonight in our county jail.") because it didn't spell out all of the hundreds of possibilities of the right's exercise? Moreover, if Story felt that presidents couldn't even be arrested or imprisoned for criminal acts (except, of course, after successful impeachment proceedings), Story must have intended that the president be immune from far less serious civil lawsuits against him arising out of his unofficial conduct. If that's not enough to show Justice Story's intent, the Court itself, in *Nixon v. Fitzgerald*, after first quoting Vice President John Adams and Senator Oliver Ellsworth (both of whom, as delegates to the Philadelphia Convention, were framers of the Constitution) as saying during the first Congress that a "President, personally, was not . . . subject to *any* [court] process whatever," offers support for that all-inclusive language by saying in the very next sentence that "Justice Story, writing in 1833, held it implicit . . . that the President must be permitted to discharge his duties undistracted by private lawsuits."

There is a related public interest in favor of the president's getting a postponement of the Paula Jones case. The president represents this nation and its image in the world community more than anyone else, by far. If his image suffers, as will inevitably happen if this case proceeds to trial, even if he prevails, so too does that of this nation. Anything that diminishes him automatically diminishes our country in the eyes of the world. *This is a public interest that the president's lawyers failed to argue or even vaguely allude to.* It alone, and quite apart from the public interest that the president be able to perform his duties undiverted by a private lawsuit, is another, very substantial public interest that infinitely outweighs the right of Paula Jones to have her lawsuit tried right now.

Can you imagine how it will play in the world's press when all of Paula Jones's graphic and lurid sexual charges against the president, told in repellent detail, come from the witness stand? No matter what is taking place in the country at the time, the testimony will be the lead story on the evening news and the next morning's headlines. Everything else will have to take a backseat. I can easily foresee the trial igniting such a vast and deafening media explosion by the world press, and the situation getting so out of hand because of sensational allegations and new and damaging revelations that the president has to respond to, that he might become more than substantially distracted by the lawsuit. Rather, he will be so consumed by his political survival that he will lose the ability to shepherd the affairs of state.

To compound the salaciousness of it all, Jones, to corroborate her assertion that the president exposed himself to her, alleged in her federal complaint that there were "distinguishing characteristics in Clinton's genital area," which she can identify (and reportedly did in a sworn May 1994 affidavit), and her lawyers can be expected to ask the trial court to order the president to subject himself to photographs of this area of his anatomy. One of Jones's original lawyers, Joseph Cammarata, was asked by CBS's Bob Schieffer on *Face the Nation* (June 1, 1997), "Are you going to require that the president be photographed in order to prove these allegations?" Cammarata: "Well . . . is [Clinton] going to admit that he engaged in the conduct Paula Jones alleges? If he doesn't, the federal rules provide for medical exams of parties. So we would request the court provide some sort of a medical exam." ABC News reporter Nina Totenberg, recognizing the outrageousness of all this, said on *Nightline* (May 27, 1997): "You simply cannot have a president of the United States answering questions under oath about his sexual conduct, about the character of his genitals, and those are clearly the questions that these lawyers are going to ask."

Since, if Jones is correct about the "distinguishing characteristics," it will indeed tend to support her allegations (but not eliminate the possibility that her alleged encounter with the president was consensual), the court may very well order the photographs. What "distinguishing characteristics" is Jones referring to? This has been the subject of whispered speculation among the media for months, with the only limitation being the fertility of the speculator's imagination. But in October 1997 several magazines and newspapers, including *Newsweek* and the *New York Times*, reported that the president's lawyer, Robert S. Bennett, had obtained a copy of Jones's affidavit through the pretrial discovery process in late September, and sources close to the case had confirmed that what Jones is referring to is, as the *New York Times* put it, "a distinctly angled bend visible when the penis is erect," a condition known as Peyronie's disease, which afflicts a not insignificant number of males. In an article titled "What Paula Saw" in the October 10, 1997, *Legal Times*, Stuart Taylor Jr. writes that "we will be treated next summer to the spectacle of a trial exploring . . . whether the President of the United

States, when in a certain state of excitement, is . . . afflicted with an eye-catching curvature of the . . . well, let's just call it the pumpkin, in light of the imminence of Halloween, and the unavoidable phallic connotations of so many other colorful fruits [and] vegetables . . . for the alleged instrumentality of harassment." Can any American concerned about the dignity and stature of the office of the presidency fail to be very concerned about this presidential peep show taking us to previously unimaginable depths of public revulsion, vulgarity, and offensiveness? The *New York Times'* Maureen Dowd said it well: "Journalists are reserving their rooms in Little Rock [this] May for a circus that promises to put previous low points in American history to shame."[24] And the photos (or, if not, the testimony of women who have known Clinton intimately in his life— Gennifer Flowers? Dare we say it, Hillary Clinton?—to confirm or rebut the "distinguishing characteristics" allegation), even though probably under court seal, will be about as easy to suppress as stopping rain from falling, inevitably surfacing in tabloids and elsewhere. Can you imagine the jokes and skits on Jay Leno, Letterman, or *Saturday Night Live*? Clinton, and therefore indirectly our country, will become the laughingstock of nations throughout the world. And our nation's citizens will undoubtedly be consumed with discussion on the trial and the unfolding drama, as tawdry and ugly as it will be. But none of this matters, of course, to the U.S. Supreme Court. Come hell or high water, Paula Jones's *individual* right to go to trial *right now* takes precedence over all other considerations affecting this nation and its millions of citizens.

On legal grounds, as well as on grounds of logic and common sense, this case should have been resolved in favor of the president's position. It should not have even been a close call. Even to seriously debate the merits of it is to lend Paula Jones's effort to have her case heard right in the middle of the president's term of office a legal dignity it does not have. This case is a why-even-talk-about-it, you've-got-to-be-kidding case.[25] Yet all nine members of the Supreme Court, without one lone voice of dissent, signed on to an opinion that gives logic a bad name, whose illogic is matched only by its silliness, one that elevates clichéd, platitudinous reasoning to vertiginous heights. It's a ruling that no rational person, after sober reflection and after becoming aware of existing legal principles, can agree with. If one can't see how wrong and absurd this decision by the Court was, then probably nothing anyone could say would make a difference. As Louis Armstrong once said when he was asked for a definition of jazz, perhaps America's only indigenous art form, "Man, if you don't know, I could never tell you."

To the question by some diehard—"How could the Supreme Court, the highest court in the land, be wrong on the law?"—my answer is that the question presupposes that the Supreme Court is always right, a notion that is not only fatuous on it face, but one that even the Supreme Court itself doesn't believe. If they did, they would never overrule prior decisions of theirs, which they not infrequently do. Note 7 of this book sets forth just a few of the many cases where the Supreme Court reversed one of their own earlier decisions. The fact that the decision in the Paula Jones case was a unanimous one doesn't change the fact that it was an incorrect ruling. If fifty million people say a foolish thing, it's still a foolish thing.

It should be added parenthetically that if the Supreme Court in the Paula Jones case did not want to declare an absolute rule of temporary presidential immunity, it could have enunciated a rule that "in all but the most exceptional cases" there should be a temporary immunity. In other words, there would be a *legal presumption* of temporary immunity, which the plaintiff, in any lawsuit against a sitting president, would have the burden of overcoming by demonstrating there was a compelling need for immediate relief. This would not be unlike the presumptive privilege for presidential conversations and correspondence established in *United States v. Nixon*, and which was overcome in that case by, the Court said, "the need to develop all relevant facts [in a *criminal* case] . . . The ends of criminal justice would be defeated if judgments were to be founded on a partial or speculative presentation of the facts."

In a *civil* lawsuit, which the Paula Jones case is, what type of "exceptional" cases would arguably overcome the presumption of temporary presidential immunity because of the compelling need for immediate relief? Perhaps a case involving child custody or alimony payments. Certainly Paula Jones's situation would not qualify. How could she demonstrate a need for immediate relief when she herself waited just two days shy of three years to even file the lawsuit? Her reply to this is that it wasn't until a January 1994 article ("His

Cheatin' Heart," by conservative journalist David Brock, the author of the 1993 book *The Real Anita Hill*) in *The American Spectator* magazine that her reputation was sullied. The article is about Clinton's alleged philandering while he was governor and how that philandering was aided and abetted by Arkansas state troopers. There is a brief reference in the thirteen-page article to a girl named "Paula," who, after spending about an hour with Clinton at the Excelsior Hotel in downtown Little Rock, told the state trooper who had taken her to Clinton's hotel room (unnamed in the article, but obviously Danny Ferguson) that "she was available to be Clinton's girlfriend if he so desired." What Paula Jones says she wants now, above all, is not money, but her good name back. However, it should be noted that not only didn't the article mention her last name, but it appeared in a small, conservative publication that most people had never heard of. Since any friends and relatives of hers who may have, perchance, come upon the article presumably wouldn't have believed it anyway, because she was not "that type of girl," who else in this entire land would she have had to worry about? If she hadn't filed her lawsuit amidst a splash of self-generated publicity and gone public with her charges, she would have remained completely unknown to 99.99 percent of the American people. Instead, she's become a household name.

So at least as to her current notoriety, doesn't she have only herself to blame? She alone made her name public. In other words, "Yes, I myself created the need for the immediate cleansing of my good name, so now I want immediate relief" is, as they say in law school, trying to pick yourself up by your own bootstraps. Stuart Taylor Jr., in the November 1996 edition of *The American Lawyer*, wonders whether Jones and those supporting and advising her are "seeking something more than to clear her good name. They did, after all, create a national scandal to rebut a single paragraph buried deep in a long story in a right-wing journal—a journal that had not even mentioned 'Paula's' last name. . . . The predictable effect has been to generate a huge wave of publicity far more damaging to Jones's reputation than one small paragraph in *The American Spectator* could possibly have been."[26]

My active interest in this case began when I started to read about it and listen to discussions about it on television. Though, as I indicated, I am not a constitutional scholar or even one who practices constitutional law, I knew and remembered very clearly from my constitutional law course in law school that whenever a public interest is in conflict with a private one, the courts (not just the Supreme Court) invariably balance the interests. I kept waiting to hear or read some reference to this in regard to the Paula Jones case, but there was absolutely no mention of it anywhere. Eventually I ordered the opinion of the Court, written by Justice Stevens. Surely it would be *there*, I told myself. But it was not. Next I ordered Robert Bennett's legal brief to the Court, submitted on August 8, 1996, over nine months before the Court's decision. Incredibly, I found *just one sentence* in Bennett's entire forty-seven-page brief where balancing of interests was even mentioned, and that was secreted way back on page 40. As I've pointed out, his whole argument was based on separation of powers.

With respect to Justice Stevens's opinion of the Court in the Paula Jones case, on the central issue of whether her lawsuit should be postponed, unbelievably (I can think of no other adverb), you're not going to find one single solitary word addressing itself to the balancing of interests. One might say, who the heck is the author of this book—who by his own admission is not a constitutional scholar or even an appellate lawyer—to say that the U.S. Supreme Court was wrong in this case because they failed to balance the interests? For starters, this is defective reasoning, and the type that great numbers of people regularly engage in. Common sense tells us that everything in life—not some things or most things but everything—has to sink or swim on its own merits, not on its background or reputation. Irrespective of authorship, what one says either makes sense and is persuasive, or it is not. Just as a wise man can say a foolish thing, a fool can say something wise.

But quite apart from these realities, would such cynics of the position taken in this book be silenced if a current U.S. Supreme Court justice said the same, precise thing I am saying about the necessity of balancing the interests? Justice Breyer, in his concurring opinion to the opinion of the Court written by Justice Stevens for the other eight members of the Court, noted that *all* immunity cases "ultimately turn on an assessment [of] the threat that a civil lawsuit poses to a public official's ability to perform his job properly. And whether they provide an absolute immunity, a qualified immunity, or merely a special procedure, they ultimately *balance* consequent potential *public* harm against *private* need." Right, Justice Breyer. That's what I recall from law school, and that's what this little book of mine is all about. Breyer, curiously speaking only in the abstract, went on to say that the distraction for a president caused by a private lawsuit justifies a postponement of the suit. But Breyer was determined to outdo his brethren in absurdity. After writing a sixteen-page opinion that, by and large, disagreed with the other members of the Court, he suddenly in the very last paragraph did a complete about-face by saying: "Yet, I agree with the majority that there is no automatic temporary immunity and the President should have to provide the District Court [the trial court] with a reasoned explanation of why the immunity is needed. . . . [I]n the absence of that explanation . . . postponement of the trial date [would be] premature." Justice Stevens, in the main opinion, said essentially the same thing. Stevens wrote that "other than the fact that a trial may consume some of the President's time [What? Other than that, Mrs. Lincoln, how was the play?]" there was "nothing [presently] in the record" to indicate that going to trial now would conflict with the president's schedule.

When one reads moonshine like this, one wonders whether they heard or read right, and if so, whether the declarant's mind has taken leave of his body. Although the president's lawyer inexcusably did not argue to the Court that balancing of interests required a postponement of this case, one thing he and the solicitor general's office did do more than adequately is set forth (to the district court, the court of appeals, and eventually the Supreme Court) why the enormous duties and singular demands of the president's job required a postponement. Even if they hadn't mentioned this fact at all, the Supreme Court could have taken judicial notice that the job of the president is, at a very minimum, among the busiest and most demanding jobs on earth. In fact, Stevens himself wrote about the Court's "recognition of the singular importance of the President's duties," and that the Court had "no dispute" with the characterization of the presidency as having "responsibilities so vast" that its occupant had to "devote his undivided time and attention" to it. Breyer, in his concurring opinion, spoke of a sitting president being "unusually busy." For Stevens and Breyer to then go on to say *there's nothing in the record* to show that a trial would conflict with the president's schedule is absolutely incomprehensible. If the past (the history of the presidency) is no guide to the future, what is? Under Stevens's and Breyer's reasoning, no one should ever prepare for anything, since you don't *know* you're going to need something until you actually do, and at *that* time you can do what's necessary. Maybe that's why Hitler, despite the fact that Russian winters are notoriously brutal, sent his troops out, without winter clothing, in his 1941 eastern offensive toward Moscow, resulting in thousands of them freezing to death. You know, how could Hitler have known that *this* winter was going to be so cold?

Since the Court accepts *absolute* immunity for judges, prosecutors, legislators, and the president himself for lawsuits against them arising out of their *official* acts, in which cases the lawsuits are automatically dismissed, why would they demand that the president, for much lesser temporary immunity, not only proceed to trial but, on a day-to-day basis, satisfy the trial judge that he has things he must do "that conflict, your Honor, with jury selection tomorrow." (Such as a summit meeting with Yeltsin, or a meeting with some recalcitrant congressmen just before a vote on the balanced budget amendment, or an emergency session with his National Security Council to decide whether to invade some terrorist nation in the Mideast that has just seized a hundred American hostages; you know, unimportant matters like this.) "Son, you may live in the White House and have all these Secret Service Agents surrounding this courthouse, on rooftops and all, but I've seen a lot more sunrises than you, and everyone hereabouts knows that this is my courtroom. Although you may have a fancier title than I do, during this trial, your ass is mine." (Just joking, of course. Actually, the trial judge in Little Rock, Susan Webber Wright, is a year younger than the president and in the mid-seventies was a student of his in an admiralty-law class he taught at the University of Arkansas School of Law. Although she's a Republican, appointed by President Bush, and campaigned against Clinton when he ran for Congress in 1974, she has thus far, particularly in her original decision to grant a postponement, been respectful of the president and his office.)

There were only two other allusions by the Supreme Court in this case to the balancing-of-interests test. The first was a one-sentence preliminary observation by Justice Stevens that the district court judge in Arkansas had used the test in granting the president a postponement.

The only other reference was in the oral arguments before the Court on January 13, 1997. And it was not only a very fleeting reference by Justice Anthony M. Kennedy, but it was so incorrect and so lacking in legal and intellectual sophistication as to almost defy description. First of all, Justice Kennedy never even mentioned any public interest at all, a *sine qua non* to a discussion of balancing interests. However, he did say: "When we talk about . . . [presidential] immunities, we're talking about balancing of interests, the rights of the [private] litigant, the necessities of the President." (One hundred percent correct so far, Justice Kennedy.) But then he immediately proceeded to say what he felt the interests in this case were that had to be balanced—and it's nothing short of shocking, considering this is coming from someone sitting on the highest court in the land. "Here, it seems to me," he went on, "[the interests to be balanced are] that the President, during the course of the stay that this proceeding produces, is free with his staff and resources to continue to argue his case, to ruin the reputation of the plaintiff, to poison the well any way he can, just as the other parties might try to do against him. But he is in a very dominant position . . . and I know of no compensating balance mechanism to protect the plaintiff."

Did you get that? He's saying that the president could defame Paula Jones more than she could defame him. This, of course, flies straight into the teeth of what has occurred here. Paula Jones and those supporting her have publicly attacked the president much more than he and his people have attacked her; the latter, for the most part, being reduced to a defensive, sometimes counterpunching role against Jones's allegation that the president sexually assaulted her. (Perhaps their most famous assault on Jones being James Carville's "If you drag a hundred dollars through a trailer park, there's no telling what you'll find." But far more important, who is defaming whom the most has absolutely nothing to do with, and is several light-years away from, the legal doctrine of balancing the public interest against the private interest. Discourse like this, coming from a Supreme Court justice, is simply embarrassing.

(A short note about Justice Kennedy, a well-respected and non-ideological jurist. It is well known in the legal profession that many judges, upon ascending the bench, think they are three steps closer to God. Some don't even recognize that limitation. And federal district court judges (which Kennedy was before his appointment to the high court) are notoriously even more insufferably pompous than their state counterparts. When one is not, he prompts this type of remark: When Kennedy was nominated for the U.S. Supreme Court in 1987, Ronald Zumbrun, the director of the Pacific Legal Foundation in California, said, "If you picture a federal judge, he does not fit it. He has a low ego threshold and he has no airs about him. *He is a normal person.*")

Since the Court did not balance the interests in the Paula Jones case, what in the world does the case stand for? The proposition—a new constitutional doctrine—that all rights and interests in our society have to be evaluated, in a given case, in an isolated fashion, a vacuum; that is, never in the context of, or relation to, other rights and interests? For instance, Uncle Smitty, who bought his little home, now a crumbling shack, fifty years ago on the outskirts of town, before the area became, like it is now, part of a thriving metropolis, and has lived there ever since—the last ten years alone, without his wife, Olive, who passed on—doesn't have to sell his little hut to the city, which is building a much-needed freeway that's going to pass right through Uncle Smitty's lot. "I know my constitutional rights," Smitty will tell you, "and the Constitution gives each citizen, if they have the do-re-mi, the right to buy property. Dadgum, with that right is the right to live, for Pete's sake, *in* your home *on* that property. Who in the hell do these people at city hall think

they are? They can go fry an egg or jump in the lake, for all I care."
One of old Smitty's cud-chewing friends told him he should have
one of his children get in touch with that big-city newspaper in
New York. They'll put the city, those sum-bitches, in their place.
They'll tell them a thing or two.

Smitty, of course, under the law of eminent domain, *will* be
forced to sell his little roost and plot of land to the city. What Smitty
doesn't know is that the real sum-bitches in this piece are the U.S.
Supreme Court and papers like the *New York Times*. Smitty doesn't
have much money, and what little he has is hidden beneath the mat-
tress of his bed and in some empty fruit jars of Olive's hidden around
his home. He's eighty-six now, with terrible arthritis, cataracts, and
emphysema, but if things get any worse, there's Medicare, thank the
good Lord, to prevent those big-city hospitals from eating up, in a
few days, everything he's saved the past sixty years, the money he
wants to leave to his kids and grandchildren. Your memory is not as
good as it once was, Smitty, but Medicare is the health plan that
wealthy, right-wing Republicans opposed years ago and have been
trying to nibble away at ever since. You see, Smitty, those people
have enough money to buy their own insurance, so why in the hell
should they help pay for insurance for their fellow citizens, folks
like you, who aren't as fortunate as they are? Anyway, Smitty, this
Democratic president, like his predecessors all the way back to FDR,
has spent a great number of hours working with his staff and certain
congressmen to prevent these right-wing Republicans—who are
conservative, Smitty, only because they've got a lot more to con-
serve than most folks—from doing this. These are the same nice
people, Smitty, who years ago, along with those boll-weevil South-
ern Democrats, opposed social security, the minimum wage, un-
employment insurance, and all the civil rights legislation in the
mid-1960s. The problem, Smitty, is that of the hundreds upon hundreds of hours this president is going to have to devote to defend
himself against this Paula Jones lady, some of them would undoubtedly have otherwise been spent thinking about ways to help folks
like you. But since the highfalutin people at that big-city newspaper
in New York think it's perfectly okay, Smitty, that the president be
tied up like this, maybe, after all, you shouldn't bother to have your
kids waste a dime calling them.

I can think of only three possibilities for the Court's failure in their written opinion, to balance the interests in this case, each of which is too rank to contemplate. Number one, the Court got caught up in the silly banalities and platitudes being mouthed by the editorial boards of the *New York Times, Washington Post,* and entities of lesser stature (about the "imperial presidency," no one being above the law, etc.), causing their collective intellect to be temporarily anesthetized and resulting in a mindless decision. This possibility takes the decision at its face value and does not read into it anything not inferable from within its pages—that is, since the Court did not say or even suggest it balanced the interests, it in fact, for whatever reason, did *not* do so. After paying lip service to an uncircumventible reality—the extreme importance of the office of the presidency—the Court went on to thereafter disregard the protection of that office by concluding they could find no legal or constitutional justification for granting immunity (e.g., separation of powers did not compel a continuance; the fact that the president has absolute immunity for official acts didn't apply here, etc.), and instead concerned itself only with the rights of Paula Jones. The Court said that a continuance of the trial to the end of the president's term "takes no account whatever of the respondent's [Jones's] interest in bringing this case to trial." The Court went on to conclude, in effect, that like any other American citizen suing someone, Jones had an absolute right to have her case tried without delay. ("Like every other citizen . . . respondent has a right to an orderly disposition of her claims," the Court said.) There's simply no indication in the opinion that they did anything other than this. Of the three possibilities, this seems the most likely, at least to me.

Number two: They knew they were required to balance the interests, and in fact did, but they also knew that if they did so in their written opinion, they'd have to rule in the president's favor, and for whatever reason, they didn't want to do that. (At least one member of the Court, Justice Scalia, an eleven-year veteran, apparently doesn't think it's beneath the Court to do such things. In a June 23, 1997, dissent of his, he wrote: "There is one more possible rationale [for the Court's] denying immunity to private [as opposed to state] prison guards worth discussing, albeit briefly. It is a theory so implausible that the Court *avoids mentioning it.*") To articulate the balancing-of-interests doctrine but then conclude that it was *more important* that Paula Jones go to trial without further delay than that the president of the United States, who represents over 260,000,000 Americans, and whose decisions affect all of us, be temporarily freed up from this very time-consuming and incredibly humiliating lawsuit would make the Court look and sound foolish and ridiculous. So to avoid appearing so, they simply did not articulate the balancing-of-interests doctrine, knowing it would take them toward a destination they did not want to reach.

To elaborate further on the possibility that although the Court never said or even implied that they balanced the interests, they in fact did, and they found Paula Jones's interest to outweigh the public interest; even if we make this assumption, this does not, obviously, exonerate them. I cannot credit the Court with balancing the interests without thereby convicting them of something even more damning. Because if this is true, their sense of importance and priorities, their sense of values and balance is so askew, so defective, that they think *one citizen's* right to have her day in court, not just eventually, but right now, is *absolute* and *more important* than the rights of the 260,000,000 people of this nation to have the office of the presidency functioning effectively every day of the year.

If the Court is indeed suffering from this type of intellectual hernia, preventing them from logical, rational thought, then I guess they would reject Justice Holmes's dictum that freedom of speech doesn't allow one to falsely shout "fire" in a crowded theater. After all, surely freedom of speech is more of an absolute right, more important and more central to what this nation stands for and is all about, than the right of any citizen to get immediate redress for alleged wrongs against them. And what would make the freedom-of-speech example in the theater even *more* attractive to the Court is that they'd only have to balance the individual right of freedom of speech against the rights of the other people in the theater, not the entire nation.

Some might say that what distinguishes the Paula Jones case from the theater case is the possible moral culpability of Clinton in this instance. Another argument might be that in the theater case, the individual did something wrong, and Paula Jones allegedly did not. But neither of these considerations changes the reality of the nation's need for the presidency to function effectively. Moreover, the courts balance interests even when the defendant *has* done something wrong. As we've seen earlier, the Supreme Court has ruled that it's in the public interest for judges, legislators, and prosecutors to have *absolute* immunity from civil lawsuits against them even if their official conduct was corrupt and malicious—even, as we saw in *Imbler*, where a prosecutor used testimony he knew, or should have known, was false and which led to the defendant's being improperly convicted of first-degree murder and sentenced to death! Conversely, even where the plaintiff has done nothing wrong at all, this doesn't save him from having his interest balanced against the public interest. What possible wrong has been done by a private citizen who wants to keep the home he lives in only to be told that under the law of eminent domain he has to sell because the city (not the nation, mind you) wants to build a freeway?[27] I know that sometimes you have to stand up for a principle, regardless of how untoward and unfortunate the result might be, because the principle is so important. But what transcendent, overshadowing principle is involved here that is so important to this nation? How important could it possibly be to this nation if Jones's lawsuit was continued to the end of the president's term? What great havoc to this nation's psyche or constitutional soul would be caused by such a decision?

The third possibility is that the Supreme Court felt that it was not required of them to balance the interests. If any readers think this is a real possibility, I would suggest they disabuse themselves of such a notion. As has already been shown in this book, whenever there are two valid interests conflicting with each other, there's only one way to resolve the matter—by balancing the interests. This is so in *all* types of cases, including presidential immunity cases, as we saw in the case of *Fitzgerald v. Nixon*.

There's no way, of course, to know which of the three possibilities set forth above is responsible for the Supreme Court's not doing, in the Paula Jones case, what a local municipal judge anywhere in the country would routinely do. It's always inherently difficult to come up with a rational explanation for something irrational.

Wherever one looks in the Supreme Court's printed decision in the Paula Jones case, one finds inaccurate statements, inconsistencies, faulty reasoning, and non sequiturs. Some examples:

• Although the Court never said that if they had thought the Paula Jones lawsuit would consume a lot of the president's time, their ruling would have been different, remarkably, they dismissed the contention that the lawsuit might be intrusive: "If properly managed by the District Court [trial court]," the Court said, "it appears to us highly unlikely to occupy any substantial amount of [the president's] time." To speak in the vernacular of this nation's youth, the Court obviously "doesn't have a clue." Quite apart from the considerable number of hours, days, and most likely weeks that the president physically will be involved in this case exclusively—meetings with lawyers, phone calls, depositions, writing notes to himself, answering interrogatories, and finally, the trial itself—anyone who has been a defendant in a civil lawsuit will tell you that it involuntarily intrudes upon your mind throughout the day, frequently takes over your life, and reduces your existence to a living hell. Justice Learned Hand, in a 1926 lecture to the Association of the Bar of the City of New York, said that a lawsuit should be "dreaded . . . beyond almost anything else short of sickness and death." This is especially true in an extremely embarrassing lawsuit of this particular nature. A few months back, there was a small article in the *Los Angeles Times* that a Sacramento jury had rejected sexual harassment and battery allegations by a woman against her onetime bosses, a California assemblyman and his top aide (but found that they had inflicted emotional distress on her). The aide responded to the jury's verdict by saying: "Mickey [the assemblyman] and I feel vindicated. This three-year ordeal was worse than anything I faced in two tours in Vietnam, including being wounded." And mind you, the charges in the Sacramento case were miles away in vulgarity and sordidness from those made by Paula Jones. Moreover, this was a case that received very little attention at all from the media, whereas *Jones v. Clinton* has already received worldwide attention.

Perhaps the readers of this book should ask themselves if, in the event they had to defend themselves in a sexual harassment lawsuit (or even a breach-of-contract, libel, or paternity lawsuit), it would adversely affect them in the performance of their job during the same period, particularly if one of the major issues at the trial was going to be whether or not there was anything unusual about their private parts. The answer, of course, is that it would. In addition to all the time the president will be forced to devote to this case, can you imagine the worry, disquietude, and anxiety over the suit and its seamy allegations that must weigh heavily on the president from time to time throughout the day, all necessarily adversely affecting him and impairing his ability to do the job he was elected to do by the American people?

• Stevens wrote that "if a trial is held, there would be no need for the President to attend in person, though he could elect to do so." This shows just how far removed from reality the Court was, making one wonder if any of them had been trial lawyers before their ascension to the bench.[28] Any lawyer worth his or her salt will tell you that it is *always* a negative, *never* a positive, for defendants not to attend their own trial before a jury. Not only is their constant involvement in the proceedings absolutely essential (all one has to do is watch a trial to see the very frequent whispering by the defendant in the ear of the defense lawyer, as well as the jotting down of information and suggestions for the counsel), but nothing can be worse for defendants than to indicate to a jury that they didn't feel the proceedings were important enough for them to bother to attend. That can only work to a defendant's detriment. With Jones suing for $525,000 (about half the president's and First Lady's net worth— Bennett has informed the media that the president's two insurance policies, which, prior to September 1997, had been paying Bennett's legal fees, will not cover any adverse judgment against the president), and since, like all presidents, Clinton is keenly concerned about his place in history, and he knows a judgment for Jones would be extremely damaging to him and represent a large, irrevocable stain on his legacy, other than his monumental presidential duties preventing him from attending the trial, what conceivable reason would he have for not wanting to be there every single day?

Not only would Bill Clinton, if he were not prevented from doing so by his presidential duties, want to be present at his trial, which, it has been estimated, will take anywhere from one to three weeks, but he would also want to be present every day of jury selection (voir dire), which the Little Rock federal judge, Susan Webber Wright, has estimated will "take about one month." You can be absolutely certain Paula Jones will be there every day throughout the entire legal proceedings, including helping her out-of-town lawyers pick individuals who she feels will be good jurors for her cause. Don't you think Clinton, who spent most of his life in Arkansas, would be able to give similar assistance to his out-of-town lawyer (Bennett, from Washington, D.C.) on the type of hometown folks he senses or feels—from their answers to questions during voir dire, as well as their demeanor and appearance—would be good for his cause? But how can he possibly take a month away from his job in Washington to spend in a Little Rock courtroom?

Bennett, in his legal brief to the Court, pointed out that "litigation [will] command a significant part of the President's time, while the urgent business of the nation [competes] for his attention. The President [will] be put to an impossible choice between attending to his official duties or protecting his personal interests in the litigation—a choice that is unfair not just to the President, but more importantly, to the nation he serves."[29]

To illustrate the conflict that Bennett was talking about, on November 12 and 13, 1997, the president's lawyers took Paula Jones's deposition for eight hours in Little Rock. The next day Jones's lawyers (with the president's lawyers present) took the deposition of Gennifer Flowers, an alleged girlfriend of the president during his Arkansas days. Lawyers who practice civil law (depositions aren't allowed in criminal cases) will tell you that many cases are won or lost *before* trial during depositions. Yet the president's schedule did not allow him to be present at these depositions, as defendants in civil cases frequently are when the main witnesses against them are being deposed. Among the many things demanding the president's attention during this same period as reported by the papers (many others the papers would not have been privy to or even attempted to report on) were these: "Congress Deprives Clinton of Money for U.N. and I.M.F. After Last-Minute Drive Fails, White House Attacks Votes as Boneheaded"; "Donation Probe Officials Question Clinton"; "Mexican President Ernesto Zedillo, Who Met with Clinton

Earlier in the Day, Joined Clinton at OAS Headquarters in Washington to Launch a Hemisphere-Wide Arms Pact"; "Clinton Imposes Import Ban on Assault Weapons"; "President Vows to Fight for Lee's Nomination to Head Civil Rights Division at Justice Department"; "Clinton Signs Bill Cutting Jobs at Two Air Bases"; etc. In addition, the president had to deal with SoDamn Insane (Saddam Hussein). These were some of the stories and headlines during this same period that Jones and Flowers were being deposed: "Iraq Expels U.S. Inspectors. Move Is 'Clearly Unacceptable and a Challenge to the International Community,' President Clinton Said After Meeting with His National Security Advisers"; "U.S. Steps Up Pressure. Clinton Sends 2nd Carrier to the Gulf"; "Former National Security Officials Under Bush Pressing President Clinton to Go Beyond Small-Scale Attacks of Recent Years"; an Associated Press photo of President Clinton on the telephone aboard Air Force One was captioned "President Confers with British Prime Minister on Iraqi Crisis."

As incredibly busy as he was, was it humanly possible for the president, during all these events, not to have images and thoughts flooding his mind off and on throughout the day—to the nation's detriment—as to what Paula Jones and Gennifer Flowers were saying at their depositions in Little Rock? And if the need arose, as it almost invariably does, how easy would it have been for Bob Bennett to reach the president, for instance, on Air Force One, or at OAS Headquarters during a break in Jones's deposition to say, "Mr. President, our friend Miss Jones has just added a new twist. She says _____." "Bob, I'll need some time to think about that. But in the meantime make sure to ask her _____."

Even if we were to assume just for the sake of argument that Clinton, as president, is entitled to no special treatment at all (because as far as this lawsuit is concerned, he's just another private citizen), what about, then, his rights as a private citizen? Is the plaintiff in a private lawsuit the only one who has any rights? Doesn't the defendant also have rights? Surely one of those rights is the right to be present during all legal proceedings against him. But Clinton, because he's president, has that right only in theory. If Paula Jones were suing another private person, that person would be in court throughout the entire legal process, as she intends to be. But

President Clinton can't possibly, for instance, take a month off from his presidential responsibilities to be present for jury selection. It's bad enough the Court doesn't feel that Clinton, even though he's the president of the United States, is entitled to any consideration at all. But should he be *penalized* because he's president?

During oral argument, Justice Souter showed how far out of it he is when he actually told Bennett that pretrial discovery "does not personally involve the President . . . I mean, the President isn't going to attend these depositions; you are." This is nothing short of unbelievable. Not only is it very common for a civil defendant to attend all important depositions of critical witnesses—where the same, identical consultation with his lawyers that takes place at the trial occurs—particularly those who give testimony in direct contravention of his position (for instance, Jones has announced she will attend Clinton's deposition), but as Bennett responded, "Don't you think that [prior to the depositions] I'm going to have to talk to the President of the United States about all of those events . . . advising [me] on what questions should be asked of witnesses? . . . I can tell you *the President has spent a substantial amount of time on this case already* [before any pretrial discovery or the trial]. . . . The very nature of this case is so personal that it would require his *heavy* involvement. . . . One has to have a sense of the extent to which someone who is involved in personal litigation can be totally absorbed by it." (As I'm submitting this manuscript, on January 15, 1998, for publication, the president's deposition is scheduled for January 17, 1998, in Bennett's Washington, D.C., office. It is expected to last between six and eight hours. As reported in the January 15, 1998, edition of the *New York Times,* "Mr. Clinton has been preparing for the deposition for several days, White House officials said, immersing himself in the likely questions of Ms. Jones's lawyers. . . .") None of these arguments was availing to the Court, however. Paula Jones was entitled to have her day in court. Now.

It should be pointed out that during pretrial discovery, the president will have to consult with his lawyers not only with respect to Paula Jones's allegations, but if the lawyers for Paula Jones get their way, he will have to work intimately with them to rebut allegations of affairs with many other women. Jones's lawyers want to introduce these alleged affairs at the trial to show a "pattern of conduct" on the president's part.

The scope of questions and areas of inquiry in civil discovery are very broad—broader, in fact, than at the trial. Under Rule 26(b)(1) of the Federal Rules of Civil Procedure, "parties may obtain discovery regarding *any* matter . . . which is *relevant* to the subject matter involved in the pending action, whether it relates to the claim . . . of the party seeking discovery or to the claim . . . of any other party. . . . The information sought need not be admissible at the trial if [it is] reasonably calculated to *lead* to the discovery of admissible evidence." The 1946 Congressional Advisory Committee's note to Rule 26 says that discovery is very expansive "to allow a broad search for . . . any . . . matters which may aid a party in the preparation or presentation of his case [at the trial]."

In the June 1, 1997, *Face the Nation* interview with Joseph Cammarata referred to earlier, he said, "We may . . . have to establish a pattern of conduct. . . . We would be looking at the relationships that President Clinton has had with other women." Bill Bristow, the attorney representing Danny Ferguson (Clinton's codefendant in the case), told trial judge Susan Webber Wright on August 22, 1997, that "enormously broad subpoenas" had been issued by Jones's attorneys for information about Clinton's alleged womanizing. On October 14, 1997, Jones's lawyers filed with the trial court their "First Set of Requests from Plaintiff to Defendant Clinton for Admissions," a list of seventy-two questions they had served on the president's lawyers for the president's answers. An example of the type asked: "Request for Admission No. 57: Please admit or deny the following: While he was Governor of the State of Arkansas, Defendant Clinton had sexual relations with women (other than Hillary Rodham Clinton), and members of the Arkansas State Police arranged meetings between Defendant Clinton and the women." Other questions concern allegations that Clinton had sexual relations with women who were "employees of the State of Arkansas" or who later became employees of the state, as well as with a woman he "later appointed to a position as a judge in the State of Arkansas."

With pretrial discovery being so permissibly broad and open-ended, it could end up being a proliferating can of very pregnant worms and become almost as involved and time-consuming to the president and his lawyers as the trial itself.

Jay Kelly Wright, a partner in the Washington, D.C., law firm of Arnold and Porter, wrote in the July 21, 1997, *National Law Journal* of his astonishment over the Supreme Court's characterization of a civil defendant as someone who is relatively detached from the litigation. Even during the pretrial phase, he writes, although "the lawyers may log more hours than the client, that does not mean that the client's involvement in the process is, or should be, insubstantial. The discovery phase of civil litigation [involves] strategic and budgetary decisions. Clients must not only be consulted, they must control the decisions. . . . For the lawyer to function effectively . . . client involvement is imperative. Moreover, the client is often a critical source of [information] and evidence, to which the lawyer needs ready access each time a significant decision has to be made in the development of the case for trial."

• In a related vein, during oral arguments before the Court on January 13, 1997, when Acting U.S. Solicitor General Walter Dellinger was making the point that a president is incredibly busy, Justice Scalia interjected: "But we see Presidents riding horseback [Reagan], chopping firewood [Reagan], fishing for stick fish [Carter], playing golf [Ford, Clinton], and so forth and so on. . . ." Interspersed with his remarks, the official transcript of the proceedings reported there was "laughter" in the courtroom. I don't know who the people in the courtroom were who found Scalia's observation so funny, but I found his asinine remark to be very offensive.

Surely Scalia knows that no matter what a person is doing during the day, whether it's dressing in the morning, working, eating dinner, driving a car, shopping for groceries, or any of the other myriad things that occupy a typical human's day, problems and events contemporaneously going on in his life continuously flood his mind. This past year I've been too busy to play much tennis, my main athletic diversion. But on the few occasions I've gone to the courts to play the game, where you're constantly in motion, and where you're concentrating on a ball coming at you at high speeds (as opposed, let's say, to the relatively stationary serenity of the golf course or sitting on a horse), thoughts kept intruding about points I wanted to make in this book and another one I am working on.

Since Justice Scalia is certainly aware of this phenomenon, one that should be too embarrassingly obvious to state, why would he make such an incredibly brainless remark? Was he suggesting that when President Clinton is on vacation and playing golf (or at any other time he is playing golf, which, he says, "relieves the pressure of the job"), none of the problems of the nation and his administration enter his mind? As President Reagan once said, "Presidents don't have vacations. They have a change of scenery." Even on vacation, of course, the president has to respond to any and all crises and emergencies facing the nation. Also, during his vacations President Clinton receives a daily national security briefing, he gives his weekly radio address to the nation on Saturday mornings, and from time to time he is seen giving speeches or talking to reporters. Even his wife is not free. When Princess Diana was killed in September 1997, who was the official representative of this nation, right in the middle of her vacation, at the princess's funeral in London? Hillary Clinton. When you and your wife, Justice Scalia, take your annual vacation, has anyone ever interrupted it by asking your wife, right in the middle of the vacation, to take two entire days off and fly across the ocean to attend some function on behalf of the United States government?

Even assuming an untruth, that during a president's vacation his mind is entirely free of the nation's problems, that he has complete rest and relaxation with absolutely no interruptions, what's your point, Justice Scalia? That the man who has the most demanding job in the world isn't entitled to a vacation the same way you are? That the citizens of this nation don't want their president to get some rest and relaxation, recharge his batteries, so he can thereafter resume his constitutional duties with renewed physical vigor? (As the expression goes, "I can give you twelve months of good work in eleven months, but not in twelve.") What's your point? Of course, you *have* no point. Your only objective, unbecoming for a Supreme Court justice while the Court was in session, was to try to be cute and sarcastic.

With respect to the infelicity of a Supreme Court justice's making a remark like Scalia's during argument on the issue of immunity for the president of the United States, readers should know that the courtroom of the Supreme Court is one of considerable stateliness and solemnity. The raised bench, where the justices sit, as well as all other furniture in the room, is mahogany. The lush draperies and carpet are a dark red. Overhead, along all four sides of the chamber, are sculpted marble panels. Directly above the bench are two allegorical figures depicting the majesty of the law and the power of government. Between them is a tableau of the Ten Commandments. To the right of the courtroom spectators is a procession of historical lawgivers of the pre-Christian era: Hammurabi, Moses, Solomon, Augustus. To the left are lawgivers of the Christian era: Marshall, Blackstone, King John, Justinian. The whole setting bespeaks an aura of solemnity, majesty, nobility, dignity. But amidst this august background, Justice Scalia, not about to let his patent on sarcasm atrophy from lack of use, added, again to laughter in the courtroom, that if President Clinton would have the "intestinal fortitude to say I am absolutely too busy [with my presidential duties to go to trial in Little Rock] so that he'll never be seen playing golf for the rest of his administration, if and when that happens, we can resolve the problem."

Let me add, by way of a very interesting footnote, that when I ordered a copy of the official transcript of the oral arguments in this case from the Alderson Reporting Company in Washington, D.C., I noticed that whenever a justice spoke to or asked a question of one of the lawyers appearing before the Court, the justice's name was not given. For instance, the transcript will read:

QUESTION: Mr. Dellinger, can I ask you about . . . ?
MR. DELLINGER: Yes.

Sometimes I could tell which justice asked the question by the lawyer's reference to the justice, by name, in the response to the question. But other times I could not. In one instance, I had to make no fewer than fifteen telephone calls over a one-and-a-half-month period to nail down for sure which justice was speaking to Mr. Dellinger as set forth on page 86 of this book. (It was Justice Kennedy, but even Mr. Dellinger, now a professor of law at Duke

University in Durham, North Carolina, couldn't recall, for sure, who it was. My original guess, from the overall context, was that it was Justice O'Connor.)[30] When I asked Bill Billingsley, quality control manager at Alderson, why the transcript was silent as to the identity of the justices, I was told that this was "a requirement laid down by the Supreme Court which is spelled out in our firm's contract with the Court." So unless you're in the courtroom at the time a justice speaks, or read a report of someone who was, you may never know who said what. I find it amazing that the justices of the highest court in the land—the protectors of our freedom of speech and expression, and of an open society—want to keep their own identity secret, not only to the citizens of this nation, but for posterity.

• The Court, in its opinion, spoke of its "recognition of the singular importance of the President's duties." But if the Court concedes the "singular" importance of the president's duties, then doesn't it reasonably follow that the occupant of the office should receive considerations that ordinary mortals do not? And shouldn't one of these considerations be that he be immune from vexatious private lawsuits so he can devote all of his time, attention, and energies to performing these duties effectively? If not, what special consideration *is* he entitled to? That his chauffeured limousine can drive through red lights on city streets?

• As stated earlier, the Court said: "As a starting premise, [President Clinton] contends he occupies a unique office with powers and responsibilities so vast and important that the public interest demands that he devote his undivided time and attention to his public duties." The Court went on to say that it had "no dispute" with the premise of that argument. But if this is so, how could they then go on to rule the way they did? Since even they later acknowledged that a trial would "consume some of the President's time and attention," did they mean that the public interest demands that the president devote his undivided time and attention to his public duties *only* during those periods when he's not physically and mentally tied up with the lawsuit against him?

Is this case just a judicial aberration, or is it ominously symptomatic of a Court on the cusp of change, one that is falling into lockstep with the increasingly insane world we live in?

Because a central theme of this book is the freakish and alarming direction in which our society seems to be going, I cannot fail to discuss a remark by Justice Stevens in his opinion. The Court wasn't satisfied with its harsh decision against the president. They had to also give him a parting shot by putting him in his place, as it were. Depreciate him. By the way, Mr. President, you may think that you're really something, but in this lawsuit you're just "[an] individual who happens to be the President" is the way Justice Stevens put it. In other words, when one thinks of William Jefferson Clinton, one *mainly* thinks of him as just some person from Hope, Arkansas, who presently resides with his family at 1600 Pennsylvania Avenue in Washington, D.C. Only secondarily do we think of him as the president of the United States. But, Justice Stevens, the person you and your eight brethren dismiss as just someone "who happens to be the President" also just happens to be the most powerful man in our entire constitutional scheme of government. One who can, for instance, take this nation to war, with the loss of thousands of American lives, and without even bothering to get a declaration of war from Congress (as, for example, in Korea and Vietnam).

Should I show you how different he is from you or I or anyone else, Justice Stevens? Let's say two scoundrels, both ex-cons, rob a federal bank in Manhattan, and not only do they get off with close to $5 million, but in the process, they kill six people—the teller, four customers—one of whom is a five-year-old girl who was being held by her mother—and a security guard. Fortunately, they're apprehended a few weeks later, brought to trial, convicted, and sentenced to death. I know you're against the death penalty, Justice Stevens, but if anyone deserves it, don't you agree these two do? Now, here's where the problem comes in. It seems that one of the robbers is a second cousin of the president, a black sheep in the family the president actually played with when they were kids. Don't ask me why, but the president has always had a soft spot for him, even though he knew he had a rap sheet thicker than a Manhattan telephone directory. Anyway, this president is a lame duck, his approval rating can't get any lower, so he decides to grant his cousin a complete pardon. And while he's at it, since he doesn't want to look like he's playing favorites, he grants the other lowlife a complete pardon, too. They're let go and are now as free as mountain goats. This is just unbelievably outrageous and terrible, of course, and the entire nation is up in arms, demanding, with demonstrations and protests, that these pardons be revoked. Folks are saying, "The Supreme Court's got to do something about this." But, Justice Stevens, as you know, although you and your brethren just love to set aside local, state, and federal laws on the ground that they are unconstitutional, there's no law here for you to set aside. What the president did was exercise a power granted to him by the Constitution itself. And although you and your people, I'm sure, have on many occasions had twitchy fingers about setting aside some provision of the Constitution, like you set aside everything else, you can't hold that the Constitution itself is unconstitutional, can you? I mean, even a bloke like me knows that wouldn't make too much sense. And the Constitution says—I don't know if you've looked at it recently, but Article 2, Section 2 [1] says—that the president "shall have power to grant reprieves and pardons for offenses against the United States, except in cases of impeachment." No ifs, ands, or buts about it. He can pardon his second cousin, and it's perfectly legal. Now, the latest (October 1, 1997) estimated census by the U.S. Census Bureau is that there are 268,234,000 of us living in this country, but only one of us, the president alone, has the power to do something like this. (The presidential power to pardon extends to people who haven't even been convicted. In *Murphy v. Ford*, 390 F. Supp. 1372 (1975), the plaintiff sought a declaratory judgment that the unconditional pardon of Richard Nixon by President Ford on September 8, 1974, "for all offenses against the United States which he, Richard Nixon, has committed or may have committed or taken part in during the period from January 20, 1969 through August 9, 1974," was void because Nixon had never been indicted or convicted, and hence, had never been formally charged with an "offense against the United States." The Court, in denying relief, said (quoting Supreme Court Justice Field in *Ex parte Garland*, 18 L. ED 366 [1867]) that the pardoning power of the president is "unlimited" except in cases of impeachment. "[The power] extends to every offense known to the law, and may be exercised at any time after its commission, either before legal proceedings are taken, or during their pendency, or after conviction and judgment . . . The benign prerogative of mercy reposed [in the president] cannot be fettered by any legislative restrictions.")

So although the president has the constitutional power to treat all of *us* completely differently than anyone else does—send us to war, pardon criminals, appoint people like you to the Supreme Court—we should treat *him* like he's no different from anyone else. Like you say, Justice Stevens, he's just someone "who happens to be the President." I've always had a sweet tooth for the symmetry of logic like that.

But the thing is, the fact that he "happens to be the President" is just what requires that we *do* treat him differently. Because of his importance to the nation, whenever the president leaves the White House a large medical van with a doctor and staff—almost a miniature hospital, with the very latest in lifesaving equipment—follows behind the presidential limousine. We permit *only* the president the right to instantaneously unleash weapons of mass destruction in self-defense against a threatening foreign power. Never far from the president when he leaves the White House is an inconspicuous and unknown military aide who carries a little black briefcase they call the "football" that contains, for the president's use only, the technology and codes to launch nuclear weapons that can incinerate a hostile nation within minutes. An entire federal agency, the Secret Service, with several thousand employees, is in existence in large part to protect the president.[31] Why, if he's not more special and important to the republic than you or I, Justice Stevens, is this so? So we want to protect the president's physical body like no other person's body in this land of ours, but according to you and your colleagues, we shouldn't have any desire to protect and shield, in any way at all, his mind, which controls his body. I see. Who am I to quarrel with such powerful logic as this?

Justice Stevens, if you're listening, to give you one final example, among a great many, of the difference to this nation and its people between anyone else, even a Supreme Court justice, and the president of the United States, even when President Clinton goes on vacation, the whole nation is informed of every little detail that a pursuing media can flush out. As I am writing this in a hotel room in

Minneapolis, the national paper, *USA Today,* is nearby, and there is a large front-page photo of the president swinging a golf club, and the front-page cover story for the day is on the president's vacation on Martha's Vineyard. On the inside page there's a small blocked-out section, amidst the long article, on "news" the White House reporters are pursuing. Question: What kind of ice cream did Clinton buy at a local shop this weekend? Answer: A double-dip of blueberry. Question: Scrabble scores for the Clintons? Answer: No answer yet. And so forth. In all deference to you, Justice Stevens, just like with me and every other single citizen in this country, no one in this country other than our loved ones cares what type of ice cream we buy. In fact, no one knows or even cares when or where we take our vacation. The reason why every known movement the president makes is covered by the media, even what type of ice-cream cone he buys, is that they know the people of this nation are interested. To characterize Bill Clinton as just "[an] individual who happens to be the President" (which, when you separate the diamonds from the rhinestones, is the essence of and basis for the Court's opinion in the Paula Jones case) not only is an insult and shows no respect for the office of the presidency, but, more personally, it's just plain silly on your part.

To suggest, Justice Stevens, that the president is no different from you or me or any other ordinary citizen is to refuse to acknowledge reality. He is. Perhaps no chief justice of the U.S. Supreme Court is revered by his peers as much as John Marshall, who served as chief justice for thirty-four years (1801–1835), the longest tenure in the Court's history. Sitting as a trial judge in the 1807 treason trial of former vice president Aaron Burr in Richmond, Virginia, when Burr's counsel sought, by way of a subpoena duces tecum (a subpoena for documents or papers), a letter from a General Wilkinson to President Thomas Jefferson (contrary to popular belief, Jefferson voluntarily complied with the subpoena, withholding only the names of individuals in parts of the letter), Marshall said: "In no case of this kind would a court be required to proceed against the President *as against an ordinary individual. The objections to such a course are so strong and so obvious that all must acknowledge them.*" To paraphrase Will Rogers, Justice Marshall never had the opportunity to meet the nine justices of the current Supreme Court.

Perhaps the Court's lack of respect for the presidency is just a reflection and culmination of the increasing lack of respect for everything in our society: the continuing decline in respect, by America's youth, for authority, even for their parents; the lack of respect for tradition; the lack of respect, as situational ethics becomes the vogue, for what's inherently right as opposed to wrong.[32]

What the condescending attitude of the Supreme Court toward the presidency further reflects is something that a lot of people already know: that the U.S. Supreme Court has gotten, for lack of a better term, out of hand. The Court, through the years, has incrementally extended its tentacles and influence over every area of American life. In wearing out several mirrors admiring the limitless power it has arrogated to itself, it apparently now feels it can look down its collective nose at the president of the United States.

As envisioned by the framers of the Constitution, the three branches of government, established in Articles 1, 2, and 3, were supposed to be *coequal* branches. Moreover, neither was supposed to usurp or even attempt to usurp the functions of any of the others. However, the Supreme Court, through its judicial activism, has trespassed many times far beyond its constitutional role of interpreting the laws enacted by Congress, becoming de facto legislators themselves, creating new laws of the land by their decisions. The hubris of judges in making law extends down to the lower courts. One is reminded of Jeremiah Smith's salty admission upon leaving the New Hampshire Supreme Court years ago to teach law at Harvard Law School: "Do judges make law? Of course they do. Made some myself." But how can the executive and legislative branches be equal to the judicial branch when the Supreme Court has become the final, irreversible arbiter not just of virtually every issue and dispute arising in our society in the course of human events, but of whether official acts of the president and legislation passed by Congress are constitutional? Doesn't that make it preeminent in the constitutional constellation? And if so, isn't this in contravention of the doctrine that the separation of powers created three coequal branches of government?

Harlan Fiske Stone, Supreme Court chief justice from 1941 to 1945, himself expressed his concern about the seemingly limitless power of the Court when he said: "While unconstitutional exercise of power by the executive or legislative branches of the Government is subject to judicial restraint, the only check upon our own exercise of power is our own sense of restraint."

The Supreme Court for the most part hears essentially two types of cases. The first is to determine if a challenged state or federal law is violative of the Constitution; the second is to determine whether a person or entity claiming injury at the hands of state or national government has had his or her constitutional rights violated. (Cases come to the Supreme Court from one or more of the thirteen federal circuit courts of appeal in the country, or from one or more of the highest courts in the fifty states.) The Court clearly has the power to resolve the second type of dispute. As to the first, not too many states'-rights advocates quarrel anymore with the Court's power to invalidate state statutes when it feels they are unconstitutional. In fact, Section 25 of the Judiciary Act of 1789, passed by this nation's first Congress, expressly gave the Supreme Court the authority to review the constitutionality of state laws. The problem is when they invalidate an act of Congress. When they do that it would seem they are, perforce, putting themselves above the supposedly coequal legislative branch of government, whose acts, under our democratic form of government, represent the will of the people of this country.[33]

Whence does the Court presume to draw such power? Admittedly, an argument could be made that the Constitution itself provides it in Article 3, Section 2 ("The Judicial power shall extend to all cases . . . arising under this Constitution [and] the laws of the United States . . . [and] to controversies to which the United States shall be a party"). However, it should be noted that Article 3, Section 2, does not *expressly* grant the Supreme Court the power of "judicial review"—the presumed power of the Court to render executive actions of the president and state and congressional legislation unconstitutional. In fact, a publication by the Supreme Court's own Office of Public Affairs titled *The Supreme Court of the United States* acknowledges on page 6 that this power "is not explicitly provided [for] in the Constitution."[34]

The opposition to this power of judicial review, although a minority view, has a rather distinguished ancestry. President Andrew Jackson said in 1832: "The Congress, the Executive, and the Court must each for itself be guided by its own opinion of the Constitution. Each public officer who takes an oath to support the Constitution swears that he will support it as he understands it, and not as it is understood by others. It is as much the duty of the House of Representatives, of the Senate, and of the President to decide upon the constitutionality of any bill or resolution which may be presented to them for passage or approval as it is of the Supreme Judges when it may be brought before them for Judicial decision. The opinion of the Judges has no more authority over Congress than the opinion of Congress has over the Judges, and on that point the President is independent of both. The authority of the Supreme Court must *not*, therefore, be permitted to control the Congress or the Executive when acting in their legislative capacities, *but to have only such influence as the force of their reasoning may deserve.*"

Jackson's view, then, was that it's one thing to have the final word on cases where an executive order of the president or congressional legislation is not involved, but when either is, the doctrine of separation of powers precludes it. In such instances the Court's decision has only that influence on the other branches which the power of its reasoning commands.

President Lincoln, in his first inaugural address (March 4, 1861), seemed to embrace this restricted view and dichotomy of the Supreme Court's powers when he said that their decisions must be "binding in any case, upon the parties to a suit . . . [and are] *entitled to very high respect and consideration* in all parallel cases by *all other departments of the government.*" He went on to muse ominously that "if the policy of the government upon vital questions affecting the whole people is to be irrevocably fixed by decisions of the Supreme Court . . . the people will have ceased to be their own rulers, having, to that extent, practically resigned their government into the hands of that eminent tribunal."

One of the greatest Supreme Court justices ever, Oliver Wendell Holmes Jr., more than once in his decisions and utterances evinced a partiality toward judicial restraint. In a speech to the Harvard Law School Association of New York on February 15, 1913, he said, "I do not think that the United States would come to an end if we lost our power to declare an act of Congress void. I do think the Union would be imperiled if we could not make that declaration as to the laws of the several states."

The notion, then, that the Supreme Court should not be able to invalidate acts of Congress (one that I am agnostic about) is not as outlandish as one may think. After all, this nation derived most of its fundamental legal architecture from the British, and in England, the judiciary does not have the power to invalidate acts of Parliament, Congress's counterpart across the water.

The most Britain has done in this area was to enact the Law Commissions Act of 1965. The act provides for the appointment of a chairman and four other commissioners by the lord chancellor (the highest judicial officer of the British Crown, who presides over the House of Lords) to the Law Commission for a term not to exceed five years. Each member of the commission must "be suitably qualified by the holding of judicial office or by experience as a barrister [British lawyer who pleads cases before Britain's higher courts] or solicitor [British lawyer who pleads cases in lower courts and helps prepare cases for barristers to try in the higher courts] or as a teacher of law in a university." The job of the Commission is to review existing laws that they feel need to be repealed or amended. They submit their "proposals for the reform of the law" in an annual report to the prime minister, who in turn "shall lay the report before Parliament with such comments, if any, as he thinks fit." When I asked a government lawyer for the Law Commission in London if Parliament has to follow these proposals, she chuckled and replied, "No, not at all. Parliament can do what they want with them, like throwing them in the rubbish bin."

If, indeed, there is a legitimate question as to whether the Supreme Court has the constitutional power to invalidate congressional legislation and executive actions; that is, if the constitutional perimeters of judicial review are not clear, should not the matter be resolved, like all disputes, by disinterested third parties, or at a minimum by representatives of the three branches of government? That's the way we resolve disputes in our society, isn't it? But setting the tone for the imperious and dictatorial attitude the Court has had for almost two centuries, Chief Justice Marshall, in the landmark case of *Marbury v. Madison*, 5 U.S. (1 Cranch) 137 (1803)—just thirteen years after the Court was first assembled on February 1, 1790, in New York City, and eleven years after it handed down its first formal, written opinion—simply declared: "It is emphatically the province and duty of the judicial department to say what the law is." In other words, "If I say so, that makes it so." And since 1803, it has been assumed and treated as a Mosaic truth with deep roots in our judicial soil that the Supreme Court—the only undemocratic branch of our government, inasmuch as it is the only branch whose members are appointed, not elected by the people—has the power to set aside decisions and actions by the other two, supposedly coequal branches of government.

Will someone, or some entity, urging judicial restraint and a policy of minimalism, challenge this assumption in the foreseeable future? For instance, will the president or Congress, in an act of civil disobedience and conscientious objection not unlike that recommended by Martin Luther King Jr. in his 1963 "Letter from the Birmingham City Jail," create a constitutional confrontation and crisis by refusing to comply with a decision of the Court? Or will the Court, in its naked judicial activism and routine invalidation of the acts of the other two branches, continue its trajectory, and if unchecked, undoubtedly expand its de facto role as first among equals in our governmental scheme? A role, one could argue, that threatens to establish a judicial aristocracy incompatible with this youthful nation's so-called experiment in democracy.

It should be added by way of illuminating footnote that the Court's disrespectful and denigrating reference to the president was in keeping with earlier indications by the Court. As set forth earlier, prosecutors, judges, and legislators have absolute immunity (i.e., the Court will permanently dismiss any lawsuit filed against them) for all cases arising out of their official duties. But when the issue arose in *Nixon v. Fitzgerald* whether a president should have the same kind of immunity arising out of *his* official acts, the very same immunity the Court had already given themselves as well as prosecutors and legislators, although the majority (five) of the Court said yes, unbelievably, in a spirited dissent written by Justice Byron White, four justices argued passionately that they didn't want the president to have this immunity—again, the very same immunity the justices themselves enjoyed. As recounted earlier, Fitzgerald sued President Nixon and others, alleging he was fired from his government job in retaliation for testifying against the government on cost overruns in the defense industry. Justice White, the former football All-American, who by most accounts was a fine Supreme Court justice and a man of impeccable integrity, flipped out in his dissent to the majority opinion. Although, in the abstract, one couldn't quarrel with his argument that absolute immunity should not extend to official conduct by a president if the president "deliberately inflicts injury on others by conduct he knows violates the law" (since the aggrieved party will then have no remedy for the wrong perpetrated against him), White knew, as Chief Justice Burger pointed out in his concurring opinion to the majority opinion, that this is the precise type of immunity that the justices themselves, as well as legislators and prosecutors, enjoy. I don't want to accuse Justice White of what LBJ once accused then-Congressman Gerald Ford of—playing too much football without his helmet on—but under what conceivable theory did he feel that he and his fellow justices, as well as prosecutors and legislators, should have an absolute immunity for their official wrongs, but not the president? (White even concedes that personnel decisions—hiring and firing—"fall within the scope of [the president's] duties.") That perhaps he and his brethren are more important than the president of the United States? That President Kennedy (who appointed White to the Court) appointed White to a position higher than the one he, Kennedy, held? As Justice Burger wrote: "The . . . emphatic concerns expressed by Justice White's dissent over unremedied wrongs to citizens by a President seem odd when one compares the potential for wrongs which thousands of [legislators], prosecutors, and judges can theoretically inflict—with absolute immunity—on the same citizens for whom this concern is expressed."

Before I end this piece, I must comment upon the editorial boards of the *New York Times* and *Washington Post*, because, as I mentioned briefly earlier, they may be partially responsible for the Court's ruling in this case.

More than any other segment of the media, newspapers are there to inform us, in a depth the electronic media does not normally provide, of what is happening in the world, and to provide intelligent commentary on these events. They are the most important of the "opinion makers" in our society. Among newspapers, the two most influential, and thought to be sagacious, particularly about politics and national affairs, are the *New York Times* (per *Time*, "easily the best, most important newspaper in the country") and the *Washington Post*. At both papers, as with others, the editorial board is considered to be the elite part of the paper, that is, the elite part of a supposedly elite paper. So if the members of the editorial boards of these two papers don't know their derriere from a hole in the ground, it's downhill in the journalistic profession from them, at least logically speaking. (Or, I should say, at least that's what these two papers would want us to believe. As Howell Raines, editor of the editorial page of the *New York Times*, puts it: "If you can work here [at the *Times*] and look around at the rest of the profession, you realize that if this place disappeared, it would not be reinvented. That imparts a sense of stewardship.") Although there are obviously many exceptions, I've always felt the media is a group that more often than not doesn't even try to create the impression that they are thinking. However, that's not true of the editorial boards of papers. To the contrary, they present themselves as the intellectual cognoscenti, with special knowledge and superb insights on current events. So let's look at how the editorial boards of the *New York Times* and *Washington Post* dealt with the Paula Jones case before and after the Supreme Court's ruling on May 27, 1997. I think I'll be able to demonstrate to you how intellectually effete these elites are, making one vapid observation after another. Suffice it to say they do not benefit from scrutiny.

For starters, as I've stated earlier, both the *New York Times* and *Washington Post* early on took the position that the president wasn't entitled to any different treatment under the law than you or I, because "presidents are, in the first instance, citizens, no more above the law than other citizens" (*New York Times,* May 25, 1994) and "The president is not above the law" (*Washington Post,* January 10, 1996). But as we've seen, the president was not claiming he was above the law, only requesting that his case be continued. So here we have the

Times and *Post* editorial boards resorting to a tired cliché, which was not even applicable here, as the basis for their opinion. I wonder, by the way, if these ardent earls of egalitarianism ("No one is above the law") have ever, even once, editorialized in favor of the thousands of plaintiffs throughout the years whose civil lawsuits against soldiers and sailors and other military personnel have been continued, *without their consent,* until the defendant soldier's or sailor's tour of duty was up?

To Robert Bennett's prediction that if the Court were to allow the case to proceed it might spawn a flood of other lawsuits against the president and his successors, the *Times,* in its May 25, 1994, editorial, said that if this prediction "about a mass of intrusive lawsuits proves correct, Congress can remedy that with legislation [immunizing the president against such lawsuits]. Until then, the broad principles of equal justice . . . cannot be sacrificed." What? What did you say? That if there are *too many* lawsuits against the president, then you *are* ready and willing to abandon this core principle of American life that no one is above the law? Then you *would* be in favor of the president being put *above* the law? You silly, silly people. Didn't you say, in another editorial, that this was a "bedrock constitutional principle"? If so, how can you possibly give it up? By the way, if people in your state of New York start filing too many lawsuits against, let's say, Donald Trump, would you suggest legislation in Albany making him immune from their lawsuits? If not, why not? Why give the president any privileges or any immunity you are unwilling to give Trump? Didn't you say that "presidents are, in the first instance, citizens, no more above the law than *other* citizens"?

The *Post,* not to be outdone by the *Times,* had their own silly spin on the danger of the Court's granting the president a delay. "For the courts to shield a sitting President, even temporarily, from civil suit on matters having no connection to his official duties, would establish a *very unwise precedent,*" the *Post* said in its January 10, 1996, editorial. But the precedent the *Post* was talking about is the exact opposite of the precedent they should have been worried about: not that a host of *valid* lawsuits against sitting presidents would be filed and delayed by the courts, but that allowing Paula Jones to proceed with her lawsuit might cause nuts, as well as a president's bitter and virulent enemies, to seize on this presidential vulnerability and file *frivolous* lawsuits against future presidents. Isn't the best way to illuminate the future by the light of the past? And when we do that we see that if the Paula Jones case goes to trial, it will be the *first* trial of a sitting president in this nation's history. In fact, although presidents have responded to written interrogatories, given depositions, and provided videotaped trial testimony in lawsuits against other people, *Jones's lawsuit is the first time in American history that a sitting president has ever even been sued.* (The *Fitzgerald* case against President Nixon was filed *after* the president left office. Likewise with a case, later dismissed, against Thomas Jefferson in 1811.[35]) So this type of thing just hasn't happened before. It's *unique.* Do the members of the editorial board of papers like the *Washington Post* just write their opinions willy-nilly? Don't they have people who do research for them before they attempt to influence millions of people with their opinions from on high? Again, if the *Post* editors had done their research and any thinking, they would have realized that what the Paula Jones lawsuit might very well do is put the thought of suing the president in the heads of many wackos, a thought that may have never entered their minds were it not for the Court's ruling. (And even though the suits might be frivolous, they can nevertheless consume the president's time and be very difficult to dispose of. As Justice Stevens acknowledged in his opinion, even if a lawsuit is frivolous, during pretrial motions by the defendant to dismiss the lawsuit "we are required to assume the truth of the . . . factual allegations in the complaint." Because of their nuisance value, this is the precise reason why so many frivolous, completely nonmeritorious lawsuits are settled out of court.) We cannot, naturally, predict events still in the womb of time, but it doesn't stretch credulity to believe that fierce opponents of a president, the type who would be wholly undeterred by sanctions imposed against them by a trial judge (if it is eventually determined down the line that the suit was filed for purposes of political gain or harassment), may in the future attempt to tie that president up in our court system.

In fact, although Jones herself may not have a political motivation for her lawsuit, there is little question that those behind her are playing "Paulatics." (This is not to suggest that Jones's suit has no merit; the merits of the case are not relevant to the much larger issue being discussed in this book.) The president's lawyers have alleged that the lawsuit against him was being funded by enemies of the president. Pursuant to this, on September 30, 1997, they served a subpoena duces tecum on the Paula Jones Legal Fund (PJLF) to secure, among other documents, the names of the donors to the fund. Jones's lawyers proceeded to file a motion for a protective order on the ground, as the president's lawyers put it, "of literally every privilege known to the common law, and then some," seeking to conceal the identity of the individual donors. On December 4, 1997, the trial judge directed the PJLF to turn over all the requested documents to the defense, but because of a confidentiality order ("gag order") issued by the trial judge on October 30, 1997, the "content of any written discovery" (as well as the time, date, and place of all depositions, and their content), which would include the documents identifying the donors, cannot be disclosed by the parties to the lawsuit. Before the gag order was issued, the PJLF did furnish to the president's lawyers nondonor documents which revealed that the PJLF was being used not just to pay Paula Jones's legal expenses but for such things as her clothing and grooming (e.g., $2,000 for clothes and hair care for media appearances during one week alone after Jones filed her complaint), jewelry, a personal computer for Jones, even care and boarding of her pet dog during a trip of hers to Arkansas, and her large public relations operation, listed as "consultants, media presentation, telemarketing, press secretary, press releases," and so forth.

The political right, indeed, is descending upon the president in the Paula Jones case, and in decidedly perverse ways. Remarkably, in May 1997, Judicial Watch, a conservative legal group, sued Clinton and State Farm Insurance Company, demanding that Clinton be forced to return to State Farm the money the company had paid for his legal defense, because, they said, legal fees for sexual harassment and defamation claims were not covered by the policy. Actually, defamation (but not sexual harassment) was covered, and shortly after the defamation count was dismissed against the president in late August 1997, State Farm and Clinton's other personal liability carrier, Chubb Group Insurance, advised the president that they would no longer be paying for his legal fees. The lawsuit was dismissed against the president but is still in the courts against State Farm.

Also, the Free Congress Foundation, an archconservative group headed by Paul M. Weyrich, a very vocal Clinton critic, has actually started running ads on radio and cable television asking women who may have been sexually harassed by Clinton to call their 800 number with the information.

President Clinton's enemies, and the far right, have actually been actively involved with the suit almost from the beginning. As reported by writer Stuart Taylor Jr. in *The American Lawyer*, Jones's first lawyer, Little Rock solo practitioner Daniel Traylor, sought the help of Cliff Jackson, another Little Rock lawyer and a longtime Bill Clinton nemesis who had earlier been retained by two Arkansas state troopers to "help them peddle their stories about their roles in Clinton's sexcapades." With Jackson choreographing everything, Jones first went public with her allegations (before she filed her lawsuit) in Washington, D.C., on February 11, 1994, at a meeting of the Conservative Political Action Conference, a right-wing organization. Taylor, a distinguished legal writer who has become the leading journalist on the case, writes that when Jones and her husband did not get sufficient attention from the mainstream media, they "wandered into the welcoming arms of conservative activists and the Christian right, which was beating a path to their door. They agreed to be videotaped by producers for far-right televangelist Jerry Falwell for what turned out to be a scurrilous video called *The Christian Chronicles* [which accuses Clinton, among other things, of being behind several murders in Arkansas as well as being a major drug trafficker]; Jones also appeared on Pat Robertson's *700 Club* show on the Christian Broadcasting Network and was interviewed by conservative . . . critic Reed Irvine on his cable television show."

In fact, as reported in a publication of the Democratic Alliance for Action, the Legal Affairs Council of Fairfax, Virginia, another right-wing group, gave Jones $4,000 to help defray legal expenses in filing her lawsuit against Clinton. The Legal Affairs Council is headed by Richard Delgaudio, the chief fund-raiser for Jesse Helms and Oliver North. Jones's two main lawyers the past few years, Gil Davis and Joseph Cammarata, are both registered Republicans. They withdrew from the case on September 9, 1997 (after a disagreement with Jones—their proposal to try to settle the case for $700,000 without an apology from Clinton was rejected by Jones),[36] and were replaced on October 1, 1997, by the Dallas law firm of Rader, Campbell, Fisher and Pyke. The firm was recruited to represent

Jones by the Rutherford Institute, a conservative religious-rights group based in Charlottesville, Virginia, whose primary source for fund-raising is evangelical Christians. Jones's lead attorney, Donovan Campbell, Jr., is the treasurer of the group. The institute's founder and president, John Wayne Whitehead, himself a lawyer, once represented Jerry Falwell's Liberty University. (The Rutherford Institute's cofounder, Jerry Mims, succeeded Falwell as head of the now-defunct Moral Majority.) Whitehead has announced that his nonprofit group, which enjoys tax-exempt status, is now paying for all of Jones's legal expenses, and has sent out by direct mail 800,000 copies of a personal letter from Jones appealing for money. Since the contributions are tax-deductible, this raises the disconcerting and incongruous specter of the federal treasury, and hence the American taxpayer, being used to help finance this private lawsuit against the president.

Going back to the *Washington Post*: In its editorial of January 10, 1996, the paper said that Jones's lawsuit was "bad news . . . for everyone concerned about the dignity of the office [of the presidency]," having earlier said in a December 30, 1994, editorial that the lawsuit "could harm Mr. Clinton *and his office severely.*" None of this, however, deterred the *Post* from concluding in its January 10, 1996, editorial: "Nevertheless . . . President Clinton is not above the law [and] Ms. Jones . . . has the right to her day in court."

The drivel from the *Post* and *Times* gets even better. (It's best to be sitting down when you read this next part, because it could literally affect your physical equilibrium.) In its May 29, 1994, editorial, the *Post*, their silliness in full flower, said: "*No matter how important it is* that the President be able to conduct the business of his office . . . like every citizen who finds himself in a legal dispute, the President must defend himself in court." In other words, apparently ("No matter how important it is"), even if the security of every citizen of this country is at risk, Mr. Clinton has to forget about his constitutional responsibilities as commander in chief of this nation's armed forces and go down to Little Rock for the trial. My, my. Even if one *wanted* to accept such mindless bilge, how could one do it without tying up and gagging one's intellect first?

But we've just begun to explore the shocking simplemindedness of the *Post* and the *Times*. They had many more rich inanities up their Brooks Brothers sleeves. The Supreme Court, in its ruling against the president, mentioned only one specific harm that might be sustained by Jones in the event of a trial postponement, and it was one of the things that the Court was most concerned about in its desire to protect Jones's individual rights. "Delaying the trial," Justice Stevens wrote, "would increase the danger of prejudice resulting from the loss of evidence, including the inability of witnesses to recall specific facts, or the possible death of a party." However, in this case, neither side has indicated there's any physical evidence that might be lost or destroyed, and the crux of the case is Jones's word against the president's. If there was an encounter between the two of them, only they, and they alone, know what happened. As far as the testimony of other witnesses, Jones says that when she left the governor's room she returned to the registration desk at the hotel and immediately told Pamela Blackard—who worked with her at the desk—what the president had done. She said she then left the hotel and went to the workplace of her close friend, Debra Ballentine, telling her the same thing. Blackard and Ballentine are perhaps the two main witnesses Jones intends to call at her trial. Both have already confirmed to many reporters, including Michael Isikoff of the *Washington Post* and *The American Lawyer*'s Taylor, what Jones says she told them. Blackard has also been on national television (ABC's *Prime Time Live*, June 16, 1994) confirming what Jones had told her, and both Blackard and Ballentine signed affidavits in February 1994 in Little Rock detailing what Jones told them. Not only is it very unlikely that they would forget the essence of what she told them (assuming their testimony would not be inadmissible hearsay), but even if they did forget, their previous statements could be used at the trial by Jones's lawyers to "refresh their memory."[37]

So the routine, formulaic objection to delaying the trial, employed almost verbatim by all parties to every lawsuit when they oppose a delay, simply would not apply in this case with anywhere near the same force as in many other cases. But even if it did, the immense public interest would overwhelmingly outweigh these considerations. As far as the death of a party is concerned, under that fear no case would ever be continued. But if the Court nevertheless had all these fears, they could have preserved Jones's rights by allowing discovery to proceed without delay—thereby eliminating their main concern about her rights—and just postponed the trial. Even that would have been very bad for the president, since pretrial discovery would consume too much of his time (and hence, under balancing of interests, should be impermissible). But the Court wasn't willing to do even that, deciding there would be no compromise. *Everything,* discovery and trial, had to proceed *during* Clinton's presidency.

As stated earlier, the district court in Little Rock had previously ruled on December 28, 1994, that although the trial against the president should be postponed until the end of his presidency, pretrial discovery, such as written interrogatories and the depositions of all witnesses and parties to the lawsuit, including the president, could proceed *during* his presidency. The trial court said that its ruling "eliminates the problem" that witnesses may forget things, and so on. Since this was the *only* specific harm cited by the Supreme Court that a delay could cause to Paula Jones and the trial court's ruling eliminated it, who could possibly complain? I'll tell you who: the editorial board of the *New York Times.* Its December 30, 1994, editorial said the ruling gave "Mr. Clinton more leeway than . . . any defendant deserves." Unbelievably, the *Times* went on to say that the trial court had "cut the President too much slack" and said the "higher courts should reject" the trial court's ruling. In other words, we don't care how important the president's job is. We don't even care that the main problem of a delay would be solved. Don't give the president anything at all. Nothing. You incredibly silly people. The frontiers of your silliness can't even be seen from Mount Palomar. I could pick five people at random at a cabstand or local Rotary Club meeting, and after some reflection they would not write such utter tripe. You should be ashamed of yourselves.

More proof that we're dealing with some very, very mediocre minds on the editorial boards of the *Times* and *Post*: In their May 28, 1997, edition (the day after the Supreme Court's ruling in the Jones case), the *Post* congratulated the Court, adding that the president's request for a continuance "carries no special weight because of his office," that is, the president's request for a postponement due to the demands of his office should not be given any more consideration than if Paula Jones were suing the local grocer. And this is the mentality of the editorial board of the *Washington Post*, the paper whose editorials not one of our representatives in Washington would even think of not reading every morning. It's as if all of a sudden the *Post* editors decided to believe that no one in our society ever gets any kind of special treatment or privileges. That it's something unknown in America. And if we ever did give anyone any special treatment or privileges at all, obviously the president of the United States would be the very last person we'd ever dream of giving it to. Hmmm. Just for starters, I wonder if the *Washington Post* is aware that under Article 1, Section 6 [1] of the U.S. Constitution, it is provided that all members of Congress "shall in all cases, except treason, felony and breach of the peace, be *privileged* from arrest during their attendance at the session of their respective Houses and in going to and returning from the same."

One more example and then we'll move on. The *New York Times* was beside itself with glee over the Supreme Court's ruling, rhapsodizing to its readers in its editorial glow the following day that the Court's ruling was not only correct, but it was the "high point of the [Court's] current term." A week later, Paula Jones's lawyers told the media that to show a "pattern of conduct" on the president's part they might seek out other women alleged to have been sexually involved with Clinton. The president's lawyer, Robert Bennett, responded that two could play that game and implied that if Jones's lawyers did this, his side might retaliate by bringing up at trial Jones's prior sexual history (relevant in that loose morals on Paula Jones's part, if any, could affect her reputation and determine if she had been defamed, and if so, to what degree). But the *Times*, in its June 3, 1997, editorial would have none of that. "All may be fair in love, war and lawsuits, but not all tactics are Presidential," the *Times* admonished Bennett. Moreover, such a retaliating tactic "ill serves a client [the president] who has espoused feminist principles and received a strong vote from women." What alligator dung.[38]

All of the *Times* editorials on the Paula Jones case in favor of a denial of the president's request for a postponement were premised on the assertion and belief that the president should be treated no differently than the average citizen. "Presidents are, in the *first* instance, citizens," they assured their readers. But when Bennett suggested that he might respond in kind to Jones's lawyers' tactics, suddenly, in the eyes of the *New York Times*, Bill Clinton the average citizen was back to being president again, and they scolded Bennett. So now the president, if we're to follow the tortuous and adolescent logic of the *Times*, not only isn't entitled to receive any special treatment by virtue of his being the president, but *because* he's president, he's not allowed to defend himself as effectively as he could if he were a private citizen. I get it.

What to make of the editorial boards of the *New York Times* and *Washington Post*, these barons of buffoonery, sultans of silliness, dukes of duncery? Are they flaming populists intent on bringing about a perfectly geometric equality in our society, even if achieved by *reductio ad absurdum* and with the price paid being harm to the republic? Or are they serious, intelligent evaluators of the social and political scene? If the Paula Jones case is any indicator, they clearly are not the latter. As for the former, both papers have exhibited a hell of a lot more elitism than populism throughout the years. In fact, their collective noses are usually so far up in the air they can touch the belly of any cloud. Then how does one account for the unmitigated blather they disseminated in the Paula Jones case? My take is that to some extent these two liberal newspapers were trying to cater to the political right in our society. But the main factor that drove their editorials, in my opinion, is that they are nothing more or less than very mediocre people who are members of a profession that, for the most part, can always be counted upon to do a minimum of thinking.

Earlier in the book I spoke of the influence of the *New York Times* and *Washington Post*. The September 29, 1997, edition of *Time* magazine said: "Even if you don't read the *New York Times*, you read it—via the TV newscasts and local newspapers that get their cues on the day's important news from the *Times'* front page. A *Times* morning-after analysis of a Presidential debate can set the agenda for days of campaign coverage and punditry. Its decision to feature, say, a murder in Texas on Page 1 can prompt hordes of reporters to hop a plane south. Its critics can make or break a Broadway play or turn an obscure foreign film into tomorrow's hot ticket." I speculated that the media (particularly the *New York Times* and *Washington Post*) and public opinion may have influenced the Supreme Court, perhaps subliminally, in its decision in the Paula Jones case. After having made this observation in the first draft of this book, I checked out of the local library Chief Justice William H. Rehnquist's book *The Supreme Court: How It Was, How It Is* (1987). In it, he writes about the case of *Youngstown Sheet and Tube Co. v. Sawyer*, 343 U.S. 579 (1952), which was decided when he was a law clerk for one of the justices who decided that case, Robert H. Jackson. As we shall see, the words I wrote in the first draft may have been coated with too much restraint.

Without getting into the merits of the case, when the United Steel Workers of America, CIO, unable to settle a dispute with the steel companies over terms and conditions in a new collective bargaining agreement, gave notice of a nationwide strike set to begin on April 9, 1952, President Truman, to avert the national catastrophe that he felt would result from a stoppage of steel production in the middle of the Korean War, issued an executive order directing the secretary of commerce to take possession of and operate most of the nation's steel mills. The steel companies appealed, and the Supreme Court decided to hear the case. Rehnquist writes that all nine justices, "eight of [whom] had been at one time or another active in Democratic politics," had been appointed to the high court by either President Truman or President Roosevelt. Rehnquist felt that the Court would uphold the constitutionality of Truman's act. "The law on the equitable issues," he writes, "was clearly in favor of the government, and while the law on the constitutional question was more or less up for grabs, the whole trend of the Court's decisions in the preceding fifteen years leaned toward the government. Why then," he asks, "did six members of the Court vote against the government in this case," resulting in the president's order being declared to be in excess of his executive authority and hence unconstitutional?

Although I found Rehnquist's answer refreshingly candid, in fact astonishingly so, I was also deeply troubled by it. Remarkably, he writes: "I think [the steel seizure case] is one of those celebrated constitutional cases where what might be called the tide of public opinion suddenly began to run against the government, for a number of reasons, and that *this tide of public opinion had a considerable influence on the Court.*" He writes about how the newspapers of the time denounced Truman's action, and how the justices had read these views in the (editorial sections of the) *New York Times* and *Washington Post*.[39] He spoke also of Truman's firing the revered General Douglas MacArthur the previous year for crossing the thirty-eighth parallel in

Korea, and the fact that the president's "standing in public opinion at the time of the Steel Seizure Case was at its nadir."

I thought the chief justice had already said quite enough, but he went on to eliminate all possible ambiguity as to the effect, in his mind, public opinion has on the decisions of the highest Court in the land. He writes: "These are the factors [public opinion, Truman's unpopularity] that I think played a considerable part in the way the Steel Seizure Case was decided. I was recently asked . . . whether the Justices were able to isolate themselves from the tides of public opinion. My answer is that we are *not* able to do so, *and it would probably be unwise to try.* We read newspapers and magazines, we watch news on television, we talk to our friends about current events. No judge worthy of his salt would ever cast his vote in a particular case simply because he thought the majority of the public wanted him to vote that way, but that is quite a different thing from saying that no judge is ever influenced by the great tides of public opinion that run in a country such as ours. Justices *are* influenced by them, and I think that such influence played an appreciable part in causing the Steel Seizure Case to be decided the way it was."

It is nothing short of mind-boggling that the highest court in the land may be deciding some cases not on the merits or the law but on public opinion. As if that's not bad enough, think of the truth of what the newspaper publisher in Ayn Rand's book *The Fountainhead* said: "Public opinion is what I make it." The situation becomes even more indecent and obscene when we realize that the only—I repeat, only—qualification for owning a newspaper (and thus becoming the principal *single* molder of your community's present and future) is having enough money to buy the paper. *Nothing else is required.* It must be added that a newspaper's political and philosophical leaning substantially mirrors that of its owner. In fact, show me one that doesn't and I will personally build a monument to that owner.

I find Rehnquist's words rather scary. Yes, we have a democracy, but in a democracy the will of the people is supposed to be expressed through their duly elected representatives in our nation's capital and state capitals throughout the country, not through national opinion polls, and certainly not via headlines and the evening television news. It may be an inevitable consequence of human nature that the justices may very well be unconsciously influenced by public opinion, as well as by the major newspapers of the land. What I find particularly disturbing about Rehnquist's remarks is that instead of making a conscious effort to resist this possibility, there is a strong implication in his words that he smilingly yields to it. If we are to take Rehnquist at his word, one wonders if the newspapers and public opinion had more of a hand than I originally thought in the Supreme Court's disregarding not only the law but simple common sense in reaching its decision in the Paula Jones case.

Nothing is more important to the high and mighty in this country (which certainly includes the members of the United States Supreme Court) than what the *New York Times* editorial board has to say about them; Rehnquist, in his book, speaks of "the justices who regularly read the *New York Times*." With the *New York Times*, buttressed by the *Washington Post*, letting the Supreme Court know in no uncertain terms that in their mind this was a no-brainer case and they wanted the Court to rule against the president, and, by necessary implication, if the Court didn't, the nine justices wouldn't be thought too highly of—as in the Steel Seizure Case, the papers (and public opinion) may have been the villains in this unfortunate decision, and the members of the Court their knowing or unknowing agents.

It should be noted that the position of the *Times* and the *Post* in the Paula Jones case was not out of the ordinary. Writer Jeffrey Toobin, in a November 3, 1997, article in *The New Yorker*, noted that the Supreme Court opinion "drew wide praise for reflecting the bedrock American principle that no one is above the law." Papers throughout the land applauded the Court's decision—*Los Angeles Times*: "A unanimous Supreme Court has ruled, correctly, that a President has no constitutional claim to temporary immunity"; New York *Daily News*: "When all is said and done, history will remember that the Court held that the President is first and foremost a United States citizen, subject to the law like everyone else. The rest will just sell soap. Cheap soap, at that"; *Miami Herald*: "This decision is a good reaffirmation that the law applies to all"; the conservative *Wall Street Journal* could hardly contain itself in its joy over the ruling: "This to be sure is an explosive matter for Mr. Clinton, [and the question is] whether this one event, the Paula Jones case, will do lasting political damage to the President. More than fair enough . . . The Clinton Presidency has asserted that it's beyond the reach of, not accountable to or immune from all manner of established processes in government. . . . If balance [among the branches of government] is preserved, American history will owe a debt to Paula Jones." Again, my, my.

Many of these same papers lamented the decision, saying it was unfortunate and would harm the presidency, but said that the Court had nonetheless ruled correctly. For instance, the *Los Angeles Times* said: "The prospect of a civil trial of a President on sex charges and the damaging consequences not just to the individual but to the institution he embodies ought to give even Clinton's most committed political enemies pause." The *Miami Herald* observed: "The Presidency, no matter who the occupant is, must not be tied in knots by lawsuits."

This sense that the opinion was unfortunate but the Court was nevertheless correct was a view articulated by a great many, including lawyers, law professors, and columnists. An editorial in the *National Law Journal* (June 9, 1997) said that the Supreme Court's decision "holds dangers for the U.S. presidency and for the U.S. political system itself" but concluded that the "Court's ruling in *Clinton v. Jones* makes . . . legal sense." The editorial board of the *New Jersey Law Journal* (June 23, 1997) said: "The Supreme Court's rejection of the President's separation of powers argument for immunity from private lawsuits may have been proper. . . . The Court may not have had any choice but to state this very Democratic (and Republican) sentiment. Even so . . . the President, be he or she Republican or Democrat, is the only one we have. If he or she becomes crippled, even marginally . . . we all lose." Famed criminal defense attorney Gerry Spence, on *Rivera Live*, said about the decision: "I'm sitting here feeling bad, Geraldo . . . and it worries me a good deal. . . . The president is the guardian of the world . . . [and] we have all kinds of international and national issues that demand his attention." But, Spence added, "Every American citizen has a right to be heard, and merely because somebody is the president of the United States, they're not cloaked with any special privileges."

Walter Shapiro, political columnist for *USA Today*, wrote that what the Court's ruling portends for the president "should make us all feel a little embarrassed to be Americans," and "no president deserves the humiliation of this lawsuit." But, he added, "I have no quarrel with the Supreme Court decision. The principle that no one, not even a sitting President, should be above the law is embedded in our legal system." Harvard law professor Alan Dershowitz, although very worried about the damage to the "dignity of the office" that a trial in this case will cause, nevertheless felt that "the Supreme Court got it just right in ruling that President Clinton has no constitutional immunity, as Chief Executive, from responding to a lawsuit brought against him by Paula Jones. Our President . . . is not above the law."

Alan should have known better, but at least he doesn't teach constitutional law at Harvard. But I find it inexcusable that his colleague at Harvard Law School, Laurence Tribe, who *does* teach constitutional law, presents oral arguments before the U.S. Supreme Court almost on a regular basis, and is perhaps the most prominent constitutional lawyer in the country, would also blindly buy into this nonsense. In the September 1997 edition of *George* magazine, after "lamenting" the fact that the president may be forced to trial by the Court's decision, he adds that he nonetheless "agrees with the Court's ultimate conclusion . . . It is a basic axiom of our Government that no one is above the law, not even the President, and it follows that no special privileges should attach to whomever holds that august office."

It is hard to even comment on the observation of someone like Tribe, who either never read the decision or, if he did (which I assume he did), must have read it far too quickly. As even the Court, in its opinion, acknowledged: "[The president] does *not* contend that the occupant of the Office of the President is 'above the law,' in the sense that his conduct is entirely immune from judicial scrutiny. The President argues *merely* for a postponement of the judicial proceedings." And yet Tribe is mouthing, like those who have no reason, as he does, to know better, that the heart of this Court's decision was that "no one is above the law." What makes Mr. Tribe's post-ruling comments even more inscrutable is that *before* the Court's decision in the Paula Jones case he signed his name to and submitted, along with fifteen other constitutional law professors around the land, an amicus curiae brief to the Supreme Court on August 8, 1996, *in support* of the president's legal position. Although it was anything but a powerful brief and took the balancing-of-interests test more for granted than arguing it forcefully, it concluded that the "nature of the Presidency necessitates that the person occupying that office be free from the diversion of energy and distraction from duty that defending such a private damages action would cause."

And in an earlier June 13, 1994, appearance on *Nightline* with former attorney general Ed Meese, who opposed any postponement of the trial, after host Ted Koppel introduced frequent guest Tribe by saying "He favors delaying the case against the president until he's out of office," Tribe proceeded to sound like me in this book. Some excerpts: "It's absolutely vital that the president not be burdened, any president not be burdened, by these kinds of distractions in office"; "Under our constitutional system, the task of balancing the plaintiff's need for an immediate day in court [against] the debilitation on the executive is a task that properly falls to the judicial branch." What should the result of that balancing be in this case? "I think, in a case like this . . . the appropriate adjustment is temporary delay, temporary immunity"; "It's the office of the presidency which needs to be protected, not Nixon, Clinton, not Reagan, not Bush"; "There is no pressing urgency that demands having a sitting president respond to a suit for damages of this sort."

What new thing Tribe learned about constitutional law between signing the amicus curiae brief in August 1996 and his article in *George* in September 1997, I can't imagine.

It should be stressed that this book is not an examination of the quality and excellence, or lack thereof, of the United States Supreme Court. It is an examination only of its decision in the Paula Jones case, with necessary journeys, here and there, to other decisions of the Court. I therefore cannot say, or do I suggest, that the Court's terrible decision in this case is an accurate microcosm of the Court's quality. The problem is that I cannot say or suggest that it is not, either; that it is a mere dandelion among the orchids. I *can* say that the Court's ruling in the Paula Jones case was so demonstrably and egregiously wrong that, like a clock that strikes thirteen times, it throws into question everything else these particular nine justices have done. Not being a Court-watcher or constitutional scholar, nor having the time or desire to be, I'll have to leave this exploration to others.

With respect to the Paula Jones decision being egregiously wrong, we all know that there is wide latitude within which others can act or think without our questioning their behavior or thinking processes. That is, we accept conduct or thinking that we ourselves could never be a party to, because it is still within the "normal" range of rational human behavior. But when others trespass beyond these outer margins into the Looney Tunes area, it raises our eyebrows, and their credibility in everything they do thereafter (and have done previously) almost necessarily becomes suspect in our eyes. This is how I unfortunately now feel about the present U.S. Supreme Court, which has lost altitude in my mind.

I speculated much earlier that the reason for the Supreme Court's irrational decision in the Paula Jones case was that the germ of craziness in our society had somehow infected the members of the Court, if even in a small way. After all, the Court, at bottom, mirrors our culture, and there's a growing pathology in our cultural foundations. We live in a society whose internal compass, at least in my mind, no longer points to true north. To suggest that the Court is not reflective of our culture *in any way* is to embrace the premise that although the Court's members come *from* our culture and were at one time pedestrian members *of* it, with their appointment to the high court they mysteriously metamorphosed into an alien body whose umbilical cord to the culture that spawned them has been clipped. But whether or not such a nexus, as tenuous as it might be, in fact existed in this case is irrelevant to the conclusion that I believe is compelled by this book—that the Supreme Court's decision in the Paula Jones case was clearly a wrong one.

Coming back full circle to the first chapter in this book where I set forth several examples of the absolute craziness that pervades our society, wherever we look, we're surrounded and engulfed by madness and insanity. The recent extraordinary convulsion of media attention given Princess Diana's death is, I think, a good example. What conceivable, *valid* reason could there possibly be for an estimated two and a half billion people, almost one-half the world's population, watching her funeral, and for her to make the cover of virtually every magazine in America and around the world, many, like *Time*, *Newsweek*, and *People*, actually publishing additional commemorative editions on her life? (Britain, of course, literally collapsed in an overwhelming outpouring of shock and grief. This is the same Britain that booted Churchill, one of the giants of the twentieth century, out of office right after he led them through the Second World War. Churchill's wife, Clementine, was found to be selling his paintings near the end of her life to survive.) The *entire* front page of the *Los Angeles Times*, as well as other major papers, was devoted to her funeral, the type of massive coverage previously reserved only for epochal events such as the end of a world war or the assassination of a president. All major networks sent their anchors to London to cover the funeral live. Together with all the worshipful reverence and adulation heaped upon Diana (and the pilgrimage to London for her funeral by dignitaries from around the world), her death was treated like a seminally historic event, almost of biblical proportions.

But *why*? It's amazing how the media tried mightily to justify it. She was a princess, a member of English royalty, they pointed out. Maybe I move in a curious circle, but no one I associate with has ever, ever, in all my years, brought up the royal family, even once, in conversation. I couldn't give a whit as to what the queen and her family are up to. Whatever it is, it's of monumental irrelevance to me. Starting with the Reform Act of 1832, the British Crown has evolved today into an institution with a largely ceremonial and advisory role, devoid of any real power. And Diana wasn't even a member of the royal family anymore.

Ah, but they say, she was also "very beautiful." And she was a compassionate woman who lent her name and devoted time to many charities and humanitarian efforts, such as those for the homeless and the victims of AIDS. From what I have since learned of Diana, she did seem to be a wonderful, compassionate human being with a warm and pleasant personality, and I certainly commend her very highly for all of her endeavors. But before her divorce from Prince Charles, she apparently was known mostly as a clotheshorse. And in the few years or so thereafter she devoted by far the lesser part of her time to these very worthy causes, the rest of the time spent pursuing a life of pleasure flitting from one tony haven for the rich and famous—Saint-Tropez, Sardinia, the south of France—to another. I repeat, I think her involvement in these charities was wonderful, but again, what's the point the apologists are trying to make? That if a famous person who was involved in charitable work dies, the entire civilized world should stop and mourn? Well, Mother Teresa, the "Saint of the Gutters," dedicated over fifty years of her life ministering, every waking hour, to the sick, the dying, and the poorest of the poor, and when she died, within days of Diana's death, her death never received anywhere near the attention that Diana's did. It should be noted that there are literally thousands of medical professionals and lay volunteers the world over who devote *all* their time and energies to caring for the poor and infirm, and when they pass on, their deaths receive about as much attention as a new fly in the forest.

Don't get me wrong. I felt very bad about Diana's tragic and untimely death. But I feel very bad whenever I read in the paper that anyone, particularly a young person such as Diana, has been murdered or died in a car accident. (For instance, in a fiery highway crash near Lompoc, California, just a week after poor Diana's death, eight young Mexican immigrants, returning in their van from a day of hard labor, collided head-on with a Ford pickup, and all eight were killed. Most came from a dusty little village of extreme poverty in Mexico where people live in small huts with dirt floors and no bathrooms. The immigrants had come to this country to earn money to send back to their families in Mexico.)

There would appear to be only one reason for the Diana phenomenon: an irresponsible press in conjunction with so many people, including the media, being celebrity-worshipers. And it is no defense for the press to say, "We gave Diana all this attention because this is what the people want." This argument smacks of rank hypocrisy. It is the precise charge that the mainstream press makes against the tabloids, whom they look down on. Moreover, if the press had covered Diana's death in a responsible manner, who would have complained? Does anyone really believe "the people" would have protested and taken to the streets, demonstrating outside the newspaper offices and TV network headquarters of America or flooding the nation's media with a massive torrent of critical phone calls and letters? Of course not. In any event, I don't believe for a moment that the media gave the colossal coverage it gave to Princess

Di's death to give the people what they want. I personally believe that most of them felt the coverage was warranted. As the *Washington Post*'s Sally Quinn said on television to support her position that Diana's death merited every bit of the media attention it received: "This story had everything."[40] Well, it certainly had you, Ms. Quinn. "Diana is certainly the biggest story of the year—no question about it," said Maynard Parker, the editor of *Newsweek*, whose magazine wasn't satisfied with one cover story on Diana. Or even a second one. They had to have a third one, the commemorative edition devoted entirely to Princess Di. And then, to make sure no one could accuse them of slighting Diana, they put her on the cover for a fourth time. Diana, simply, was someone whom the world could no longer do without. Indeed, the mythologizing and apotheosis of Princess Di prompted by her death induced two academics, planning a university course on her, to proclaim breathlessly that Diana had emerged as "the modern Virgin Mary, the saint of women."

Sarah Ferguson, the Duchess of York, says her sister-in-law, Diana, would be "amazed" by the incredible reaction to her death. "She'd say, 'No. Go on. You've got to be kidding.' " I would think any sensible person watching the media become totally unhinged in their treatment of Diana's death would have said the same thing to the media—"You've got to be kidding."

The response to Diana's death was just another manifestation of the fact that the much greater part of mankind hears only the music, not the lyrics, of human events, and much of society today is crazy, almost certifiably so. And when I hear about someone jumping off the merry-go-round and fleeing to some remote cabin in the mountains to live, safely away from the assaults upon their sensibilities delivered daily by newspapers, radio, and television, I understand why.

For those who elect to remain in the frenetic maelstrom we call modern life, what's the moral of the Supreme Court's decision in the Paula Jones case? It's pretty clear: In the madding crowd of contemporary America, where nonsense, incompetence, and bizarre behavior seem to now be the norm, all of us who consider ourselves to be rational and sane have to realize we're navigating through society's tempestuous waters virtually alone. That there apparently is no longer an intellectual port in the storm, a commonsense anchor we can look to for succor and reassurance. And if we ever find ourselves ensnared in a legal jam, we might be a helluva lot better off if we happen to be a buck private going through basic training at Fort Benning, Georgia, than if we're the president of these United States.

I mean, if we can't look to the United States Supreme Court as an island of sanity in this increasingly crazy society of ours, is our nation morally and intellectually adrift, without moorings, and subject to whatever capricious wind might blow? It is, of course, a rhetorical question.

NOTES

1. Although the prosecuting attorneys' incompetence in the Simpson case was of a staggering nature, incompetence of a lesser degree among trial lawyers is so common that I *expect* it. However, there is an extremely strong myth in our society—the origin, I imagine, being from novels and films—that trial lawyers, particularly defense attorneys on big cases, are brilliant, great, high-powered, silver-tongued; that they're magicians, able to pull rabbits out of hats, and so forth. Although there is incredible incompetence wherever one looks in life, for some curious reason, because of this myth, trial lawyers are perceived to be an exception. The reality is that the overwhelming majority of trial lawyers in jury trials are either incompetent or operating at a very low level of competence. And if most prominent trial lawyers met their reputations out on the street, they wouldn't recognize each other. Yet the media persists in automatically attributing to lawyers on big, high-visibility cases abilities they do not have.

For instance, in the Simpson case, the press immediately started to refer to Simpson's defense team as the "best that money can buy" and the "Dream Team," but I pointed out in a national magazine interview before the trial that this was Robert Shapiro's very first murder trial; Johnnie Cochran was mostly a civil lawyer, not a criminal lawyer, and had apparently never won one single murder case before a jury in his entire thirty-two-year career; and F. Lee Bailey, of course, had lost the last big case he tried, over twenty years earlier—the Patty Hearst case, considered in the legal community to be a very winnable case. And as I established very clearly by many examples in my book *Outrage*, Cochran, Shapiro, and Bailey (as opposed to the two DNA lawyers from New York, Barry Scheck and Peter Neufeld) were spectacularly ordinary during the Simpson trial itself, prevailing for reasons that had nothing to do at all with any legal brilliance on their part.

I give many examples in *Outrage* of incompetence in our society. Just one: When you move into a brand-new home, aren't there usually a hundred defective things, many of which require your calling the workers out three or four times to fix once and for all? But these carpenters, plumbers, electricians, and so on are not morons. They are perfectly normal, incompetent people. It is just too much for them to do their job well, even though the work they do is relatively simple work they do every day, and it's almost mechanical, necessitating very little thinking. I mean, a substantial percentage of people don't even know how to leave their phone number on your answering machine, speaking so fast that you have to play their message back several times just to get the correct number. If incompetence is so endemic in our society, even among people doing simple, repetitive things with a lot of time in which to do them, doesn't common sense tell you that the incompetence is going to be even more common and pronounced with trial lawyers, who deal with different witnesses in every case, with different facts and evidence, who are constantly forced to think on their feet under pressure of time, and who have an opponent who is trying to thwart and negate their every move? Yes, common sense tells one this. But this is not the way our society sees it.

2. In *Outrage*, I give many examples of this phenomenon. For instance, because I know the Special Investigations Division of the Los Angeles DA's office very rarely prosecutes police misconduct, such as brutality cases, I was surprised when prosecutor Chris Darden, in his summation to the jury in the Simpson case, said, "I spent seven years prosecuting bad policemen." Just on the possibility that I was wrong and Darden had been *prosecuting* police without me or anyone else knowing about it (perhaps in the middle of the night, with only the goblins as witnesses), I called two current Deputy DAs who worked alongside Darden between 1987 and 1994, when Darden was in SID. They both told me Darden prosecuted only one case in seven years, and it wasn't a police brutality case. It was the "39th and Dalton Street" case, a 1990 misdemeanor prosecution (unsuccessful) of several LAPD officers for physically trashing a duplex apartment house searching for drugs. And yet the *Los Angeles Times* said Darden "had long experience in *prosecuting* police officers." *Newsweek* called Darden a "cop-busting D.A." Jeffrey Toobin, in the *New Yorker*, said "Darden spent seven of his fifteen years as a Deputy District Attorney *prosecuting* corrupt police officers." Why did they say these things about Darden? Because he was in a section that was "supposed" to prosecute bad cops. Whether he actually did or not was a question that never entered the minds of these reporters. Seeing what one *expects* to see is a frailty that, for whatever reason, I don't seem to be afflicted with. Now, admittedly, that's not very modest. But then again, trial lawyers are notoriously immodest. One of my favorite stories about modesty: Winston Churchill was running for re-election in Great Britain against Clement Attlee, and a member of the British press told him, "Sir Winston, I think you'll have to agree that Mr. Attlee is a lot more modest than you," whereupon Churchill replied, "Yes, but then again, he has a lot more to be modest about."

3. Among so many other terribly unflattering things, as most know, there is no more staunch supporter of the tobacco industry—whose product, according to the American Medical Association, kills upward of 400,000 Americans every year from lung cancer— than Jesse Helms (R-N.C.). Yet Helms, chair of the Senate's Foreign Relations Committee, refused in September of 1997 to let the Senate even vote on President Clinton's nomination of former Massachusetts governor William Weld for the position of U.S. ambassador to Mexico. Helms's stated reason? Weld's support, in Massachusetts, for the medicinal use of marijuana for the terminally ill. It was an outrageous act of raw power by a petty right-wing tyrant against a sensible and well-qualified moderate Republican, yet Senator Richard Lugar (R-Ind.) was the only senator on the committee who possessed the virtue and courage to denounce Helms. Pathetic sycophants like Senator Joseph Biden (D-Md.) hardly raised a whimper. The remarkable Helms, a self-styled superpatriot, is the same person who, that same month, tried to hide in a foreign aid bill an incredible provision that would have put the claims of America's tobacco companies on $1.3 billion in frozen Iraqi assets in America *ahead* of claims by veterans of the Gulf War. Can you imagine that? When the measure was fortunately discovered, the House immediately voted 412–5 to reject it. To borrow an appellation from the past, Helms "is a sight seldom seen in Christendom."

4. Although Limbaugh has an uncontrollable passion for dishing it out, spouting his venom on Clinton and the Democratic Party every single day without letup, he's a sniveling coward who can't take it himself. To avoid all opposition or critical comments, he never has guests on his show and heavily screens all callers. There's nothing I'd like more to do—and I hereby issue a challenge to him—than to engage Limbaugh in a televised de-

bate for a minimum of two hours on a college campus or elsewhere. And if I am unable to de-limb Limbaugh, I promise to turn in my bar card.

5. Overall, Lawrence Walsh, the Iran-Contra special prosecutor, conducted his investigation with much more dignity and professionalism than Kenneth Starr. Starr, who is a darling of the Republican right wing—and this potential for bias should have automatically disqualified him from being appointed "independent" counsel in the Whitewater probe—is not, really, the Whitewater prosecutor. He's the Bill and Hillary Clinton prosecutor, hell-bent on investigating every breath they have ever taken and doing everything imaginable to get the Clintons out of the White House and behind bars for alleged crimes that didn't even happen while Clinton was president and for which the statute of limitations has long since run out. (Although there is no language expressly stating it, it is nonetheless clear that since the purpose of the Independent Counsel ["Special Prosecutor"] Act of 1978, 28 USCA §591 et seq., is to prevent the misuse of power by the president and other high-ranking members of the executive branch of government, it was intended to apply only to crimes allegedly committed while they were in office, not to those allegedly committed before they took office. Indeed, of the eighteen investigations since the Act was passed in 1978 as a response to Watergate, *USA Today*'s Susan Page—who wrote a comprehensive article on the law and its implementation—told me she believes that Starr's investigation of Clinton for his involvement in Whitewater is the first one dealing with alleged misconduct of someone *prior* to his taking office.) Among other things, Starr actually was sending out (before adverse public opinion caused him to stop) investigators to question witnesses about the identity of women with whom Clinton may have had extramarital affairs many years ago in the hope of picking up from the women incriminating "pillow talk" to aid the investigation. The out-of-control Starr took his investigation even further afield than that, demonstrating a troubling preoccupation with Clinton's private sexual life. One Arkansas state trooper, Roger Perry, told reporters last August that when Starr's investigators spoke to him originally, "I thought they were trying to get to the bottom of Whitewater. But the last time they spoke to me I was left with the impression that they wanted to show he was a womanizer. All they wanted to talk about was women. They even asked me if I had ever seen Bill Clinton perform a sexual act. The answer is no."

The "independent" counsel is supposed to be, above all else, impartial. In fact, anything that taints even the *appearance* of impartiality should automatically disqualify one from occupying the position. Impartiality is so important that sometimes they overcompensate in the selection of an independent counsel to ensure fairness. For instance, the Watergate prosecutor who helped bring about President Nixon's resignation, Leon Jaworski, was a cochairman of Texas Democrats for Nixon in his 1972 campaign for reelection. Walsh, investigating the Republican administrations of Presidents Reagan and Bush for Iran-Contra, was himself, as he said, "a Republican of fifty years' standing." Yet Starr, who is investigating Democrat Clinton, is a deep-eyed, conservative Republican who was appointed to the federal court of appeals by President Reagan, was named U.S. solicitor general by President Bush, and before his appointment as Whitewater independent counsel was seriously thinking about running, as a Republican candidate, for the U.S. Senate from Virginia. During his tenure as independent counsel, he has improperly continued to represent, for fees in excess of $1 million, large corporations (such as two tobacco companies—Philip Morris and Brown and Williamson) whose interests are antithetical to, and would obviously profit from, the failure of the Clinton administration and its policies. Reporter Jane Mayer has learned that Starr was also retained as a consultant in the summer of 1995 to the ultraconservative Lynde and Harry Bradley Foundation on the school-choice issue. This foundation has contributed substantially to entities who have promoted and featured allegations of offenses and improprieties committed by President Clinton, such as *The American Spectator* magazine and the Free Congress Foundation.

As if that's not enough, as reported by Mayer in the April 1996 *New Yorker*, "Starr had been publicly outspoken in his support for Paula Jones' contention that Clinton had no right to claim special immunity from civil suit while in office, and two weeks before his appointment [as Whitewater prosecutor] the *Washington Post* reported that he would probably be filing a supporting [amicus curiae] brief [for Jones]. . . . His appointment as independent counsel intervened before a final decision to file the brief was made."

So here we have the absolutely inexcusable situation of someone who was already a virtual legal opponent of the president being appointed independent counsel to investigate the president. The three-judge panel that appointed Starr in August of 1994 was headed by federal Court of Appeals judge David B. Sentelle, a conservative Republican from North Carolina who owes his judgeship to that paragon of fairness and moderation Senator Jesse Helms.

Starr's investigation of a very small-time money-losing real estate venture by the Clintons way back in 1978, with a large prosecutorial staff of twenty-five lawyers and the assistance of the FBI, as of this writing has taken longer than the Second World War and cost the taxpayers (per the General Accounting Office) close to $35 million, clearly at odds with the mandate in Section 593 of the Independent Counsel Act that he "conduct the investigation and any prosecution in a prompt, responsible, and cost-effective manner." To demonstrate just how outrageous the $35 million expenditure is, the 1992–93 congressional House committee that investigated whether the 1980 Reagan-Bush presidential campaign had secretly subverted the Carter administration's hostage negotiations with Iran to influence the election—a matter that could hardly be more important—spent only $1.35 million on its investigation. Yet already close to $35 million has been spent by Starr on the monument to minutiae called Whitewater. As of November 30, 1997, apart from the Paula Jones case, President Clinton and his wife, Hillary, owed $2,993,396 in legal bills, almost all of which is due to the blue-chip Washington, D.C., law firm of Williams and Connolly for their representation of the Clintons arising out of Whitewater-related matters. This is *after* a legal defense fund (now disbanded) established by friends and supporters to help pay the first couple's legal bills had already paid Williams and Connolly $1,310,447. At least on paper, then, the Whitewater investigation has already financially bankrupted the Clintons, whose net worth, per their last financial disclosure statement in May 1997, was listed as being between $760,000 and $1.7 million. The president has vowed to pay every dollar he owes from his postpresidential earnings.

As far as the Paula Jones case, all that is known is that prior to their discontinuing coverage in September 1997, the president's two personal liability insurance companies had paid, per the president's lawyer, Robert Bennett, "more than $1 million" to him in legal fees. Since September, the president himself is being billed, and estimates of future legal bills in the case have ranged from $2 million to $3 million.

6. While all this silliness was going on in the late summer and fall of 1997, Senator Fred Thompson (R-Tenn.), the chairman of the Republican-controlled Senate Governmental Affairs Committee investigating the Democratic fund-raising practices, was asked by the Democrats to investigate Republican fund-raising, too. Unbelievably, the Republican Party, particularly the right wing, strongly objected to this, wanting Thompson's

committee to investigate only the Democrats. Thompson retreated, but later carried on an extremely brief and modest (next to what his committee was doing with the Democrats) inquiry into the fund-raising of the Republican National Committee. Again, unbelievably, he was met by a strident chorus of right-wing opposition, some of whom actually called him a "traitor."

As if all of this was not insane enough, contemporaneously, Senator John McCain (R-Ariz.) and Senator Russ Feingold (D-Wisc.) proposed a campaign finance reform bill to, as they said, "reduce the influence of money on our political process and to help make sure that all Americans, not just a wealthy few, can make their voices heard in that process." Among other things, the bill would have banned all "soft" money. Unlike the highly regulated "hard" money to political candidates, corporations, unions, and wealthy people can give as much "soft" money as they want to national party organizations. That is, the McCain-Feingold bill would make unlawful the very thing the Republicans were investigating the Democrats for doing at the White House and elsewhere, and which the Republicans traditionally do more of. (For instance, in the 1996 presidential campaign, the Republicans raised $138.2 million in soft money, the Democrats $123.9 million.) But the Republicans in the Senate, led by Senate majority leader Trent Lott (R-Miss.), killed the bill. Incredibly, congressional Republicans were vigorously condemning Democrats for campaign financing abuses while simultaneously blocking meaningful campaign finance reform legislation that would prevent these very abuses. All forty-five Senate Democrats along with eight Republicans voted yes, seven votes short of the sixty needed to halt a Republican filibuster on the bill and allow the bill to be voted on. Forty-seven Republicans voted no. *In other words, these Republicans were refusing to change the very practices they were investigating.*

I have a question for these right-wing Republicans, one to which, if they respond truthfully, I already know the answer. It's a paraphrase of attorney Joseph Welch's remark to Senator Joseph R. McCarthy during the U.S. Senate hearings in June of 1954 on alleged subversive activities in the U.S. Army: "Have you people, at long last, no sense of shame?"

7. A few illustrative cases. *O'Malley v. Woodrough,* 307 U.S. 207 (1939), overruled *Miles v. Graham,* 268 U.S. 501 (1925), as to the constitutionality of taxation of salaries of federal judges; *United States v. Darby,* 312 U.S. 100 (1941), overruled *Hammer v. Dagenhart,* 247 U.S. 251 (1918), as to congressional power over labor in the manufacture of goods; *West Coast Hotel Co. v. Parrish,* 300 U.S. 379 (1937), overruled *Adkins v. Children's Hospital,* 261 U.S. 525 (1923), and *Morehead v. Tipaldo,* 298 U.S. 587 (1936), as to power of a state to enact minimum-wage laws. In fact, as recently as December 10, 1997, the Court, in *Hudson v. U.S.* (U.S. Supreme Court #96-976), ruled that a criminal prosecution, where the defendant had previously paid a civil fine for the same conduct, did not violate the double jeopardy clause of the Fifth Amendment, thus overruling their previous decision in *United States v. Halper,* 490 U.S. 435 (1989). The *Halper* decision, by the way, was, like the Paula Jones case, a unanimous decision of the Court. Chief Justice Rehnquist, who wrote the *Hudson* opinion and, it should be noted, was also Chief Justice at the time of the *Halper* decision, said: "We believe that *Halper's* deviation from long-standing double jeopardy principles was ill-considered." In other words, the Supreme Court, in *Hudson,* admitted that it goofed, made a mistake, was wrong, in *Halper.*

For a list of many more cases, see *Burnet v. Coronado Oil and Gas Co.,* 285 U.S. 393, 407–409 (1932). In *Burnet,* Justice Brandeis said: "*Stare decisis* is not . . . a universal, inexorable command. . . . Whether it shall be followed or departed from is a question entirely within the discretion of the court, which is again called upon to consider a question once decided."

8. Section 1983 derives from the Ku Klux Klan Act of 1871, enacted by the federal government during the Reconstruction era period to correct a lack of justice in the South where criminal acts by state officials against certain people—mostly blacks, but also anti-secessionist whites—were condoned by state authorities as well as all-white juries. The U.S. Supreme Court, in *Monroe v. Pape*, 365 U.S. 167 (1961), said that the failure of the former Confederate states to enforce the law equally was "the powerful momentum" behind the Act of 1871.

9. I always get a kick out of lawyers using, without explaining, legal terms like certiorari in front of laypeople as if the latter know what they mean. For instance, the word *certiorari* is obviously a word that average Americans routinely use every day—you know, "Give me a Coke and a certiorari." "How are you feeling today?" "Oh, my certiorari is killing me." A petition for certiorari is a request to the U.S. Supreme Court to hear and decide a case that the petitioner has lost either in a federal court of appeals or in a state supreme court. Ever since the Certiorari Act of 1925, the votes of four out of the nine justices are required for the Court to grant certiorari and agree to review a case. Five votes, of course, are required to form a majority ruling.

10. One often hears, for instance, people say that American citizens are entitled to be tried "by a jury of their peers." No one has yet defined precisely what this term means. Certainly it doesn't mean that serial killers are entitled to have their cases heard by other serial killers, or someone like O.J. Simpson tried by professional football players. But a definition is unnecessary, since "a jury of one's peers" is simply a term that has become a part of the American vernacular but has no foundation in American law. (The term did appear, actually, in the Magna Carta, the thirteenth-century charter granted by King John, which is regarded as the foundation for English constitutional liberty and a predecessor to this nation's constitution.) Under the Sixth Amendment to the U.S. Constitution, an accused is entitled to be tried by "an impartial jury." American case law has engrafted upon this constitutional mandate the requirement that the impartial jury be chosen from a "representative cross section of the community."

11. "There is no liberty if the judiciary power be not separated from the legislative and executive. Were it joined with the legislative, the life and liberty of the subject would be exposed to arbitrary control; for the judge would be then the legislator. Were it joined to the executive power, the judge might behave with violence and oppression. There would be an end to everything, were the same man, or the same body, whether of the nobles or of the people, to exercise those three powers, that of enacting laws, that of executing the public resolutions, and of trying the causes of individuals." Montesquieu, *De l'Esprit des Lois* (The Spirit of the Laws; 1748).

12. The district court judge in Little Rock, of course, may ultimately conclude that the president's schedule is so chock-full it's not possible to shoehorn the trial in, and hence continue the matter till after the president's term in office. The Supreme Court, although specifically rejecting in its ruling the district court's earlier decision to do this as an "abuse of discretion," could still eventually defer to the trial court's discretion in its management of the case if the latter once again, on the presentation of new evidence, concludes that a trial during the president's term is not feasible.

Also, the defense will undoubtedly make a motion for summary judgment prior to the trial. The trial judge could grant the motion and dismiss the case against the president if, after examining all the pretrial discovery and affidavits submitted by both sides, the judge concludes that Jones's case has no merit and she would not be able to prove her case to a jury.

13. Of course, a fourth possibility is the coin of the realm in diplomacy—compromise. I have found no case where the U.S. Supreme Court has used this technique to resolve a conflict between a public and a private interest. Though not denominated or perhaps even intended as such, the ruling of the U.S. District Court in Little Rock way back on December 28, 1994 (postpone trial, but not pretrial discovery), was in the nature of a compromise.

14. A case that one could argue—although I think erroneously—stands for the proposition that the Court does not have to balance two valid competing interests is *United States v. Robel*, 389 U.S. 258 (1967). Robel, a member of the Communist Party, was indicted under the Subversive Activities Control Act of 1950, which made it a crime for *any* member of a "Communist-action" or "Communist-front" organization to work in a place designated a "defense facility" (here, a shipyard in Seattle). Robel sought a dismissal of the indictment on the ground that the statute, in limiting his employment opportunities, unconstitutionally abridged his right of association, protected by the First Amendment.

The Supreme Court agreed, holding that Congress in this case had exceeded its authority to enact laws to prevent subversion and espionage in plants on which the national defense depends because it "indiscriminately" made "any" member of a "Communist-action" or "Communist-front" organization fall within its ambit. The Court said the statute made it "irrelevant to [its] operation that an individual may be a passive or inactive member of [one of these organizations], that he may be unaware of the organization's unlawful aims, or [even] that he may disagree with those unlawful aims. It is also made irrelevant that an individual . . . may occupy a nonsensitive position in a defense facility." (President Truman, whose veto of the proposed legislation had been overridden by Congress, had gone further, pointing out that "the language of the bill is so broad and vague that it might well result in penalizing the legitimate activities of people who are not Communists at all, but loyal citizens.")

In a loosely worded footnote at the very end of the decision, the Court said: "It has been suggested that this case should be decided by balancing the governmental interests . . . against the First Amendment rights asserted by the appellee. This we decline to do. . . . Our inquiry is more circumscribed. Faced with a clear conflict between a federal statute enacted in the interests of national security and an individual's exercise of his First Amendment rights, we have confined our analysis to whether Congress has adopted a constitutional *means* in achieving its concededly legitimate legislative goal. . . . In this case, the *means* chosen by Congress are contrary to the letter and spirit of the First Amendment."

I say the footnote was loosely worded because it is phrased in such an imprecise way that it could possibly be read to mean that the Court doesn't have to balance the interests in all cases. Well, it doesn't if, as in a case like this, the *means* used to protect the public interest is itself unconstitutional. Here the Court said the statute contained "the fatal defect of overbreadth because it seeks to bar employment both for association which *may* be proscribed [by Congress] and for association which may *not* be proscribed consistently with First Amendment rights." In other words, the statute itself was so defective that the Court struck it down without even having to consider the balancing of public and private interests.

But the Court made it clear that if the statute had been sufficiently specific in its language so that it would apply only to Communists who posed a threat to national security, the statute's effort to protect the public interest would have been upheld. The Court's language about the statute's barring the employment of someone for "association which *may* be proscribed" was followed by the even more explicit declaration that "Congress *can* declare sensitive positions in national defense industries off limits to those who would use such positions to disrupt the production of defense materials."

In fact, even those First Amendment cases decided in the mid-1960s by the so-called absolutists (Justices Warren, Black, Douglas, Brennan, Goldberg, and Fortas) did not reject the balancing-of-interests test at all. The justices were simply a little more inclined, at least in First Amendment cases, to balance in favor of the individual. Perhaps more important, a review of those cases reveals that the federal or state statute was determined by the Court to be itself defective (like Robel), or the government failed to demonstrate a sufficient public need for the targeted freedom of expression to be restricted, or it was clear that the individual simply had not done what was prohibited by the statute. See, for instance, *Lamont v. Postmaster General,* 381 U.S. 301 (1965); *Brown v. Louisiana,* 383 U.S. 131 (1966); *DeGregory v. Atty. General,* 383 U.S. 825 (1966); *Cox v. Louisiana,* 379 U.S. 536 (1965); and *Freedman v. Maryland,* 380 U.S. 51 (1965).

15. In criminal federal narcotic cases, the stay for companion civil forfeiture proceedings, when requested by the government, is even provided for statutorily. See 21 USCA §881(i) (1984).

16. In *Briscoe v. Lahue,* 460 U.S. 325 (1982), the Court held that all witnesses at a trial "are absolutely immune from damages liability based on their testimony."

17. A few who come to mind (and who, out of respect for their own integrity and profession, from time to time break with the party line) are George Will, William Safire (who is already on record as being in favor of a postponement of the Paula Jones case), Pat Buchanan, William Buckley (who insists on depriving himself and us of his splendid intellect by his almost predictable partisan cant), and the promising Arianna Huffington.

18. A joke going around during the Eisenhower era told of an American boasting to a Russian: "In America, I can stand in front of the White House and shout 'President Eisenhower is no good.' " "I can do the same thing in Russia," the Russian retorted. "I can stand in front of the Kremlin and shout 'President Eisenhower is no good.' "

19. One of President Franklin D. Roosevelt's favorite stories was about a wealthy businessman commuter from heavily Republican Westchester County in New York who would hand the newsboy at the train station a quarter every morning for the *New York Times,* glance at the front page, then hand the paper back as he rushed out the door to catch his train. Finally, one day, the newsboy, unable to control his curiosity any longer, asked the man why he always only looked at the front page.

"I'm interested in an obituary notice," the man said.

"But the obituaries are on the back pages of the paper, and you never look at them," the newsboy retorted.

"Son," the man said, "the son of a bitch I'm interested in will be on page one."

20. Scalia is the same justice who, in *Morrison v. Olson,* 487 U.S. 654 (1988), wrote: "Article II, § 1, cl 1, of the Constitution provides: 'The executive Power shall be vested in a President of the United States.' . . . This does not mean *some* of the executive power, but *all* of the executive power" (Scalia's emphasis). Even knowing this, it is still apparently perfectly all right with Scalia that *all* of the executive power of the U.S. government, as vested in one person, the president, be tied up for however long it takes on the Paula Jones private lawsuit, not in running the nation.

21. Stevens, in a footnote, writes: "As the court held in *Herbert Morris, Ltd. v. Saxelby,* (1916) A.C. 688, 704, the employer's interest in protecting trade secrets does not outweigh the public interest in keeping the employee in the work force." (The majority opinion in *Snepp* concluded that "vital national interests" justified the requirement that employees not publish any information relating to the CIA without securing prepublication clearance from the agency. Justice Stevens, in his dissent, balanced the other way, in favor of the employer, because the government conceded that Snepp's book contained no classified information.)

22. Excerpted from Akhil Reed Amar and Neal Kumar Katyal, "Executive Privileges and Immunities: The Nixon and Clinton Cases," 108 *Harvard Law Review* 701 (1995). Remarkably, nowhere in the article do the authors talk about balancing of interests.

23. In fact, Article 1, Section 8 (18) expressly provides that Congress shall have the authority to "make all Laws which shall be necessary and proper for carrying into execution the foregoing [enumerated] Powers."

24. Ronald Brownstein, political writer for the *Los Angeles Times*, predicts that "the circus-like atmosphere" that will surround the trial in Little Rock will "probably rival or exceed O.J. mania."

25. In author R. J. Gray's article "Private Wrongs of Public Servants," 47 *Calif. Law Review* 303 (1959), he treats the issue as an "of course" one, not even open to discussion. After asserting that a president, even for his torts (civil, not criminal, wrongs), "must be exempt from the reach of the courts" because of his capacity as head of state, he adds: "There's no reason why this immunity, though *necessary* while he is in office for acts occurring before and during his term, should extend beyond the conclusion of this term. Thus, an uncompensated plaintiff should be entitled to bring his action once the President has given up his office."

26. I should tell the reader that in 1996 Stephen Jones, Paula Jones's husband, telephoned me to ask if I would represent Paula in a contemplated lawsuit against *Penthouse* magazine for publishing nearly nude pictures of her in suggestive poses taken years earlier by a former boyfriend who had sold the pictures to the magazine. I declined for several reasons, one of which is that I don't handle civil cases. But I used the occasion to tell him my view that his wife's lawsuit against the president, even if it was meritorious and she won, may in the long term end up being more harmful than beneficial to her, and in the process would do considerable damage to the presidency. I also commented on the fact that the people behind his wife were political enemies of the president who most likely were just using her as a vehicle to further their own ends. The thrust of my remarks was that he and his wife should give some thought to dismissing the suit with a declaration that her charges were true but she was taking this action in the national interest. This, I told him, would most likely be viewed by millions of Americans as an act of nobility on her part. In the alternative, I suggested that she be amenable to continuing the lawsuit until after the completion of the president's term in office. Mr. Jones listened politely to my suggestions but was noncommittal. I got the clear impression that Jones, a ticket agent for Northwest Airlines at LAX and an aspiring actor, is much more sophisticated than his wife. I also sensed that he was, as his wife has been reported to be, for the most part apolitical.

Jeffrey Toobin, in the November 3, 1997, edition of *The New Yorker*, writes that Susan Carpenter-McMillan (a conservative Los Angeles activist for years who has become Paula Jones's close friend, confidante, and chief spokesperson, and is believed by some to be against a settlement and nudging Jones toward a highly publicized trial with the president) told him Jones had once asked her: "The Republicans—are they the good 'uns or the bad 'uns?"

Jones, the daughter of a small-town (Lonoke, Arkansas) evangelist preacher, whose parents wouldn't permit a television set in the home until Paula, the youngest of their three daughters, turned eighteen, has said about Carpenter-McMillan, who is married to a wealthy Pasadena, California, lawyer: "She's always trying to protect me. And she knows me. No one knows me like Susan." For her part, Carpenter-McMillan (who has called Clinton a "slimeball") refers to Jones as "a modern-day Joan of Arc."

27. Way back in 1878, the U.S. Supreme Court, in the case of *Boom Co. v. Patterson*, 98 U.S. 403, articulated the law of eminent domain: "The right of eminent domain, that is, the right to take *private* property for *public* use, appertains to every independent government. It requires no constitutional recognition; it is an attribute of sovereignty. The clause found in the Constitution of the several states providing for just compensation for property taken is a mere limitation on the exercise of that right."

28. All judges, of course, must be lawyers—that is, with the ironic exception of justices of the U.S. Supreme Court. Although no nonlawyer has ever sat on the Supreme Court, President Lyndon Johnson did try to get his secretary of state, Dean Rusk (not a lawyer), to accept a nomination to the Court. Rusk declined.

29. Some people have said, "Well, if the President is tied up, let Vice President Gore run the country." Number one, the people elected Bill Clinton president, not Al Gore. Second, the Twenty-fifth Amendment to the United States Constitution, ratified on February 10, 1967, says: "In case of the removal of the President from office or of his death or resignation, the Vice-President shall become President." This Amendment obviously does not contemplate the vice president's taking over if the president is in a Little Rock courtroom.

30. I finally found someone who was not only inside the courtroom, but had notes, which she read back to me, that confirmed it was Justice Kennedy. Linda Greenhouse, the Supreme Court reporter for the *New York Times*, though working on a deadline, graciously took the time to get this information for me. If I had this much trouble now, can you imagine how much difficulty a researcher would have in getting this type of information one hundred years, even ten years, from now?

31. As former Secret Service agent Dennis McCarthy writes in his book *Protecting the President* (1985): "Every minute of every day, agents are on duty protecting the President, both as an individual and as a symbol of the government that he leads." And part of their duty is to give their very life to save his, if necessary. All agents are trained, McCarthy says, "to put themselves between the President and the source of the shots." A celebrated example was when John Hinckley attempted to assassinate President Reagan just after Reagan had exited the Hilton Hotel in Washington, D.C., on March 30, 1981. McCarthy writes: "The first shot was fired when Reagan was just three feet from the limousine door that agent Tim McCarthy was holding open. Immediately, Tim turned in the direction of the shots, spread his arms and legs to protect the President, and took a bullet in the abdomen." (Tim McCarthy survived. In fact, he is presently running for secretary of state in Illinois.)

Despite being perhaps the most protected person on earth, the president still has the most dangerous job in the industrialized world. Though we have had only forty-two presidents, four have been assassinated (Lincoln, 1865; Garfield, 1881; McKinley, 1901; Kennedy, 1963), and there have been six attempted assassinations (Jackson, 1835; FDR, 1933; Truman, 1950; Ford, 1975 [twice]; Reagan, 1981). And virtually every president receives many threats of assassination. Has any Supreme Court justice (and there have been a great many more of them than presidents) ever been assassinated, or even had an attempt made on his or her life? Indeed, has even one of the thousands of senators or representatives in our nation's history ever been assassinated because of his position or performance in office?

32. A national poll of veteran teachers published in the September 9, 1997, edition of *USA Today* found 81 percent saying students have less respect for authority than they once did. Seventy-three percent found them to be less ethical and moral.

33. According to the last compilation by the Congressional Research Service, as of 1992, 135 acts of Congress had been struck down as unconstitutional in whole or in part by the U.S. Supreme Court. Among other recent cases, on June 25, 1997, the Court, in *City of Boerne v. Flores, Archbishop of San Antonio*, 117 S. Ct. 2157 (1997), held that Congress exceeded its power under Section 5 of the Fourteenth Amendment in enacting the Religious Freedom Restoration Act of 1993. The very next day, in *Reno v. American Civil Liberties Union* (discussed on pages 64–65 of the narrative) the Court invalidated the Communications Decency Act of 1996.

34. "Some also feel that the legitimacy of Judicial Review is deducible from the Supremacy Clause of the Constitution. Article VI, [2], provides that "[t]he Constitution, and the Laws of the United States which shall be made in Pursuance thereof . . . shall be the supreme Law of the Land.""

35. Three other American presidents had civil lawsuits pending against them at the time they took office, but in each case the lawsuit was filed *before* their term commenced. An action against Theodore Roosevelt and the Board of Police in New York City, of which Roosevelt had been chairman in 1895, was filed by an NYPD patrolman who had been fired from his job. The suit was dismissed before Roosevelt took office and the dismissal was affirmed on appeal while he was serving his term. A suit against Harry Truman when he was a county judge in Missouri was filed by someone who alleged that Truman and other judges had committed him to a mental institution without cause. The suit was likewise dismissed before Truman took office, and the dismissal was affirmed on appeal while he was president. A suit against John F. Kennedy in California by delegates to the 1960 Democratic National Convention for injuries resulting from an automobile accident sustained while riding a car leased to Kennedy's campaign was settled after Kennedy became president.

36. This lawsuit was almost settled, with*out* any payment of money, back on May 5, 1994, the day before Jones filed her suit. According to an October 1, 1994, press release by Jones's lawyers, whose contents, at least as to the proposed settlement language, the president's lawyers have not disputed, the lawyers for Clinton and Jones had agreed that Clinton would say: "I have no recollection of meeting Paula Jones on May 8, 1991, in a room at the Excelsior Hotel. However, I do not challenge her claim that we met there and I may very well have met her in the past. She did not engage in any improper or sexual conduct. I regret any untrue assertions which have been made about her conduct which may have adversely challenged her character and good name. I have no further comment on any previous statements about my own conduct. Neither I nor my staff will have any further comment on this matter." Jones was then to respond: "I am grateful that the president has acknowledged the possibility that he and I may have met at the Excelsior Hotel on May 8, 1991, and has acknowledged my good name and disagrees with assertions to the contrary. However, I stand by my prior statement of the events." Reportedly, these statements were acceptable to Clinton, but Gil Davis and Joseph

Cammarata, Jones's lawyers, said in the press release that they were not "completely acceptable to Mrs. Jones. [She] was pleased with the language recognizing and acknowledging her good name and character. However, she found the statement somewhat odd in that Mr. Clinton agreed to validate her conduct without acknowledging that she was *in* the hotel room with him." But they added that "Mrs. Jones was willing to continue to negotiate acceptable language. The real reason negotiations collapsed was the need for a tolling agreement [a suspension of the statute of limitations], not an insistence that Clinton admit his misconduct." (Robert Bennett, the president's lawyer, had told reporters on the day the suit was filed that negotiations had broken off because the president "was not going to apologize for something he didn't do.")

The October 1, 1994, press release by Jones's lawyers went on to say that since the statute of limitations was going to expire on their client's cause of action three days later, on May 8, 1994, they wanted a six-month extension (tolling) within which to file her lawsuit, but "Mr. Bennett [the president's lawyer] responded that Mr. Clinton wanted the case over on May 6, and that a tolling agreement was a 'deal breaker.' The White House knew that [the proposal for a] filing delay was a courtesy extended to Mr. Clinton by Mrs. Jones to allow negotiations to bear fruit. Yet 'unnamed sources' in the White House knowingly gave false reasons for the delay to the press. CNN broadcast that night [May 5, 1994] that these sources claimed that Mrs. Jones 'decided not to file after all because she realized she didn't have a case and that her family was against her.' " "That was a lie," Davis has told reporters, and Jones filed her lawsuit the next day. Another long settlement conference between Bennett and Jones's lawyers—Davis and Cammarata— took place at the offices of Bennett's Washington, D.C., law firm on August 5, 1997, but again, no agreement was worked out. (Davis and Cammarata, no longer Jones's lawyers, have filed a notice of lien for $800,000 in attorney's fees against any judgment Jones may be awarded in this case.) As this book is going to press, CBS News reported on January 11, 1998, that they had learned that Jones had almost tripled her original $700,000 demand of the president and was now only willing to settle for $2 million plus an apology from the president.

37. Not everyone confirms that Jones reacted to the alleged encounter with the president as she states in her complaint. Charlotte Brown, Jones's older sister, told a Little Rock television audience on May 5, 1994, that although her sister Paula had told her on May 8, 1991, that Clinton had propositioned her earlier in the day in the Excelsior Hotel room and that she had turned down his advances, rather than being upset about the incident, she appeared "thrilled" about it. "I don't believe in all my heart it was sexual harassment," Brown said in the interview. She added that her sister had spoken to her shortly before she left for her press conference in Washington, D.C., on February 11, 1994 (when she first went public with her allegation), and that Paula had told her "whatever way it goes, it smells money." Lydia Cathay, Jones's other sister, accused Brown of fabricating what she said: "I'm extremely upset. She's lying." Cathay said that when her sister, Paula, recounted to her the hotel encounter with Clinton, Paula was very upset and was in tears.

Mark Brown, Charlotte Brown's husband and Paula Jones's brother-in-law, has been as changeable as Kansas weather. He told Sydney Blumenthal of *The New Yorker* that "Paula's suing over a stupid lie, and she knows it. . . . [It's] because of one woman wanting to be real wealthy, to be in the movies and be on TV. This is a hell of a price to pay, a premeditated lie—by more than one person, too." But he later said he believed his sister-in-law "absolutely." Most recently, however, he was observed walking into the Little Rock courtroom in the company of the president's lawyers.

In the June 23, 1997, *Legal Times,* Carol Phillips, a former receptionist in Governor Clinton's office, told Stuart Taylor Jr. that the day after the alleged harassment episode, Jones "came by the governor's office" and volunteered in "a happy and excited manner" that "she went up to meet the governor and they met in a room and they just talked." Phillips was of the firm impression that their meeting had been "totally, totally, totally innocent." Phillips said she knew Jones well since Jones was a courier for her agency, the Arkansas Industrial Development Commission (AIDC), who made twice-daily deliveries to the governor's office. She said she and Jones "hit it off" and "would go to lunch nearly three times a week," during which time Jones would talk about her job (she hated it), boyfriend, and other "woman talk." But "after the meeting at the hotel," Phillips said, "it was totally changed. The whole conversation moved to the governor. . . . She was just in awe of this meeting. And because she and I talked of things of a personal nature—there was no shyness between us—she would have told me if anything had happened. She was just very, very excited. This was the most exciting thing that had happened to her. She was not an innocent person, but when it came to this, it was almost childlike."

Phillips said that after Jones met Clinton in the room, "she stayed longer during her daily visits to the Governor's reception area. She often asked whether Mr. Clinton was in and, if not, when he would return. She also called me on the telephone to ask when Mr. Clinton would be in his office so that she could come by when he was present. I recall her checking the Governor's parking space to see if his car was there. She was eager to see and speak with Mr. Clinton. She never expressed any fear or distrust of him, nor did she ever indicate in any way that she was concerned about losing her job at AIDC."

Phillips said that Jones "often spoke with State Troopers Danny Ferguson and Larry Patterson, both of whom were assigned to the Governor's security detail and who were present in the Governor's suite of offices. In my presence, Ms. Jones would ask the troopers questions about Mr. Clinton and his whereabouts."

Phillips told Taylor that Jones had hoped her meeting with Clinton might lead both to a better job and to a romantic relationship with him. But Jones's hopes were dashed, according to Phillips, and she began to complain that Clinton had forgotten her. At one point, when Clinton was away and "a big humongous birthday card" had been put in his reception area for signatures by his staff, Phillips said Jones asked if she could sign even though she was not on his staff. "She put a little note on there," Phillips remembers, "that said, 'Hi, Happy Birthday from Paula.' And she put a question mark on it." She described Jones as a "misguided person. She's an ambitious person. I think that someone helped her to concoct this story, because this is not the person I know."

The thirty-five-year-old Phillips admits to being an admirer of the president, but she says she did not know him well and had never been a part of his "in crowd." She now works at the Department of Agriculture in Washington, D.C., but told Taylor she had received no special treatment in landing the job.

38. As it turned out, the defamation count (count four) of Jones's federal complaint against the president—where a key issue would have been what Jones's reputation was before all of these events occurred—was later dismissed by the trial judge on August 22, 1997. But that, of course, doesn't mitigate, in any way, the indefensible nature of the earlier *New York Times* editorial attack on Bennett (June 3, 1997, over two and a half months be-

fore), when the defamation count was still extant. Moreover, the issue of Jones's reputation still remains, by Jones's own words, at the heart of her lawsuit—that she is suing not for money but to "clear my good name."

Since the trial judge, on August 22, 1997, dismissed the defamation count only against President Clinton, not against his codefendant, Danny Ferguson, the latter's lawyer, Bill Bristow, announced that he intended to explore, in depth, Jones's reputation and sexual history. In fact, Bristow deposed a witness on October 23, 1997, who testified to a sexual encounter with Jones following a high school graduation party. Negative revelations, if any, about Jones, would inevitably have redounded to Clinton's benefit as well. However, in an attempt to eliminate any legal justification for Bristow's introducing evidence of Jones's sexual history, Jones's lawyers made a motion to file an amended complaint deleting the defamation count Jones had filed against Ferguson, and on November 24, 1997, the judge granted the motion. On December 8, 1997, Jones filed her amended complaint deleting the count four defamation count against Ferguson. This greatly reduces, though it does not eliminate, the likelihood that Jones's prior sexual history, if any, will be heard by the Little Rock jury. The only other substantive change (a significant one) from the original complaint in Jones's amended complaint is the allegation that Clinton had a "predatory custom, usage and habit" of using Arkansas state personnel and resources "to solicit sexual favors," and that those women who, unlike Jones, had "succumbed to Defendant Clinton's" sexual advances were granted "directly or indirectly, governmental and employment benefits, appointments, raises, promotions, positions, and perquisites" denied to Jones because she resisted said advances, i.e., the president discriminated against Jones. The trial judge ruled that in view of this new allegation, Jones's lawyers could now not only seek out other women allegedly solicited by Arkansas state troopers for sexual liaisons with Clinton, or those he had sexually harassed, but women with whom he had consensual sex and were rewarded thereafter by Clinton with state or federal jobs or positions. As with his answer to the original complaint, in President Clinton's December 17, 1997, answer to the amended complaint, he said he "adamantly denies the false allegations advanced in the amended complaint."

39. From David McCullough's 1992 book *Truman*: "The *New York Times* accused [Truman] of acting on 'almost inconceivably bad advice.' The *Washington Post* predicted his seizure of the mills would probably go down in history as one of the most high-handed acts ever committed by an American President. . . . 'Nothing in the Constitution can be reasonably interpreted as giving to the Commander in Chief all the power that may be necessary for building up our defenses or even for carrying on a war.' "

40. The paparazzi have turned out to be the main villains in this piece, and they are, to be sure, vultures of the first water. But I find it not only ironic but a little incongruous for people, who buy magazines in large part because of celebrity photographs, to in effect be saying, "We love the photos, but hate the photographers who took them."

ABOUT THE AUTHOR

VINCENT BUGLIOSI received his law degree in 1964 from UCLA Law School, where he was president of his graduating class. In his career as a prosecutor for the Los Angeles County District Attorney's office, he won 105 out of 106 felony jury trials, including 21 murder convictions without a single loss. His most famous trial was the Charles Manson case, which became the basis of his book *Helter Skelter*, the biggest-selling true-crime book in publishing history. F. Lee Bailey calls Mr. Bugliosi "the quintessential prosecutor." Alan Dershowitz adds that "Bugliosi is as good a prosecutor as there ever was."

Both *Helter Skelter* and his subsequent *Till Death Us Do Part* won Edgar Allan Poe Awards for best true-crime book of the year. He followed this with another true-crime book, *And the Sea Will Tell*, which rose to #1 on the *New York Times* hardcover bestseller list. All three books have been adapted for network television.

Bugliosi's most recent book, *Outrage: The Five Reasons Why O.J. Simpson Got Away With Murder*, also a #1 *New York Times* bestseller, is the only book out of the over seventy on the Simpson case that was nominated for a Poe award. Dominick Dunne says: "If you only have time to read one book on the criminal case of O.J. Simpson, I would recommend, without hesitation, Vincent Bugliosi's *Outrage*." Bugliosi, who lives with his wife, Gail, in Los Angeles, California, is currently working on a two-volume tome examining the assassination of President John F. Kennedy.

Coming from

THE LIBRARY OF CONTEMPORARY THOUGHT

*America's most original writers
give you a piece of their minds*

John Feinstein

Edwin Schlossberg

Pete Hamill

Seymour Hersh

Carl Hiaasen

Anna Quindlen

William Sterling and Stephen Waite

Jimmy Carter

Robert Hughes

Susan Isaacs

Nora Ephron

Joe Klein

Donna Tartt

Don Imus

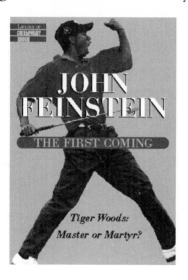